MW00605040

BIBLICAL PARENTING

From the Bible-Teaching Ministry of

CHARLES R. SWINDOLL

BIBLICAL PARENTING BIBLE COMPANION

From the Bible-Teaching Ministry of Charles R. Swindoll

Charles R. Swindoll has devoted his life to the accurate, practical teaching and application of God's Word and His grace. A pastor at heart, Chuck has served as senior pastor to congregations in Texas, Massachusetts, and California. Since 1998, he has served as the founder and senior pastor-teacher of Stonebriar Community Church in Frisco, Texas, but Chuck's listening audience extends far beyond a local church body. As a leading program in Christian broadcasting since 1979, *Insight for Living* airs in major Christian radio markets around the world, reaching people groups in languages they can understand. Chuck's extensive writing ministry has also served the body of Christ worldwide and his leadership as president and now chancellor of Dallas Theological Seminary has helped prepare and equip a new generation for ministry. Chuck and Cynthia, his partner in life and ministry, have four grown children, ten grandchildren, and two great-grandchildren.

Based upon the original outlines, charts, and transcripts of Charles R. Swindoll's sermons, the Bible Companion text was developed and written by John Adair, Th.M., Ph.D., Dallas Theological Seminary, a writer in the Creative Ministries Department of Insight for Living.

Published By:
IFL Publishing House
A Division of Insight for Living
Post Office Box 251007
Plano, Texas 75025-1007

Editor in Chief: Cynthia Swindoll, President, Insight for Living
Executive Vice President: Wayne Stiles, Th.M., D.Min., Dallas Theological Seminary
Writer: John Adair, Th.M., Ph.D., Dallas Theological Seminary
Theological Editor: Wayne Stiles, Th.M., D.Min., Dallas Theological Seminary
Content Editor: Kathryn Merritt, M.A., English, Hardin-Simmons University
Copy Editors: Jim Craft, M.A., English, Mississippi College
　　　　Paula McCoy, B.A., English, Texas A&M University-Commerce
Project Coordinator, Creative Ministries: Noelle Caple, M.A., Christian Education, Dallas Theological Seminary
Project Coordinator, Publishing: Melissa Cleghorn, B.A., University of North Texas
Proofreader: Paula McCoy, B.A., English, Texas A&M University-Commerce
Cover Designer: Dameon Runnels, B.A., Art – Mass Media; B.A., Mass Communications, Grambling State University
Production Artist: Nancy Gustine, B.F.A., Advertising Art, University of North Texas

ISBN: 978-1-57972-992-9
Printed in the United States of America

Table of Contents

A Letter from Chuck

I'll never forget that evening after my wife gave birth to our first child. As soon as I got home from the hospital, I dropped to my knees in our tiny, three-room campus apartment at Dallas Seminary and cried out to God, "Please help me know how to be a dad. Cynthia's never been a mom. We don't know what we're doing, so dear Father, please help us!"

Cynthia and our new son, Curt, came home soon after. Together, Cynthia and I took a dive into the Scriptures! God began answering my prayer slowly, revealing over time the things we needed to know as He provided direction through His Word. In the process, He rescued our children from many of the mistakes we could have made, and He gave us grace to recover from the mistakes we did make. Where we applied His principles, our children thrived.

Parenting is one of the most difficult jobs given to human beings. When God places babies in our arms, He also places us in some of the most trying circumstances we will ever face. For some parents, these challenges involve life-and-death issues. For the rest of us, they only feel that way. No matter who we are, parenting puts us in a position where we either grow and mature . . . or we wither and fade.

Parenting isn't just difficult. It is also one of the most rewarding jobs given to human beings. God uses children to fill corners of our hearts we never knew were empty. That swelling pride . . . that bubbling joy . . . these feelings have no match. God's grace to us through our children is immeasurable. What a treat!

This book, based on a series of sermons I gave called *Biblical Parenting*, walks you through the lows and highs of parenting. The lessons apply, whether you're living with preschoolers or in an empty nest . . . in fact, whether you have no children of your own or you're a grandparent with only memories. This Bible Companion covers the whole scope of what it means to be a parent. As you read, you'll encounter interactive questions to spur you to think on a variety of topics related to your own children—how God made them, how you're training them, and how to recover after having made mistakes.

Our four children have grown up and given us ten grandchildren and two great-grandchildren, and still, Cynthia and I learn more about the sorrows and joys of parenting every day. I believe this Bible Companion will encourage you to persevere in your pursuit of being a godly parent. I trust it will help you to think clearly about God's desires for parents. And I hope it will prompt you to do often what I did that first night home from the hospital . . . *pray!*

Charles R. Swindoll

How to Use This Bible Companion

Human beings are learners. We seek out topics of interest and pursue them with curiosity and attentiveness. If you've picked up this volume, you clearly have an interest in parenting. Within this study, you'll find chapters that clarify the biblical understanding of parenting and address common misunderstandings associated with parenting. You'll also find practical advice for the day-to-day life of a parent. You'll discover that each chapter interacts deeply with God's Word, allowing you to learn from the *one* truly reliable source that believers possess.

You may work through this study individually or with a group, but regardless which method you choose, a brief introduction to the overall structure of the study will help you get the most out of it.

Lesson Organization

 THE HEART OF THE MATTER serves as an introduction to each lesson, highlighting the main idea for rapid orientation.

Each lesson itself is composed of two main teaching sections for insight and application:

 DISCOVERING THE WAY explores the principles of Scripture through observation and interpretation of the Bible passages, drawing out practical principles for life.

In observation, our goal is to see what's on the page—to gather facts. We take note of key words and phrases, names and places, comparisons and contrasts, and causes and effects.

In interpretation, our goal is to make sense of our observations—to determine what's spiritually significant about the facts we've gathered. We accomplish this by asking questions about history, culture, literature, and grammar. Once we've answered these questions, we reach general conclusions about the passages of Scripture under consideration.

Parallel passages and additional questions supplement the main Scripture passages for a more in-depth study.

 STARTING YOUR JOURNEY focuses on application, helping you put into practice the principles of each lesson in ways that fit your personality, gifts, and level of spiritual maturity.

Using the Bible Companion

The *Biblical Parenting Bible Companion* is designed for individuals, but it may be adapted for group study. If you choose to use this Bible Companion in a group setting, please keep in mind that many of the lessons ask personal, probing questions, seeking to reveal true character and challenge the reader to change. Some answers may be embarrassing if shared in a group setting. Care, therefore, should be taken by the leader to prepare the group for the sensitive nature of the study, to forego certain questions that appear too personal, and to remain perceptive to the mood and dynamics of the group, redirecting as questions or answers become uncomfortable.

Whether you use this Bible Companion in a group or individually, we recommend the following method:

Prayer—Begin each lesson with prayer, asking God to teach you through His Word and to open your heart to the self-discovery afforded by the questions and text of the lesson.

Scripture—Have your Bible handy. We recommend the New American Standard Bible, The New Living Translation © 2007, or another literal translation, rather than a paraphrase. As you progress through each lesson, you'll be prompted to read relevant sections of Scripture and answer questions related to the topic. You'll also want to look up the Scripture passages noted in parentheses.

Questions—As you encounter the questions, approach them wisely and creatively. Not every question will be applicable to every person every time. Use the questions as general guidelines for your thinking rather than rigid forms to complete. If there are things you just don't understand or want to explore further, be sure to jot down your thoughts and questions.

Special Bible Companion Features

Throughout the chapters, you'll find several special features designed to add insight and depth to your study. Use these features to enhance your study and to deepen your knowledge of Scripture, history, and theology.

GETTING TO THE ROOT
While our English versions of Scripture are reliable, studying the original languages can often bring to light nuances of the text that are sometimes missed in translation. This feature explores the underlying meanings of the words or phrases in particular passages, sometimes providing parallel examples to illuminate the meaning of the inspired biblical text.

DIGGING DEEPER
Various passages in Scripture touch on deeper theological or prophetic questions. This feature will help you gain deeper insight into specific theological issues related to the biblical text.

DOORWAY TO HISTORY
Sometimes the chronological gap that separates us from the original author and the original readers clouds our understanding of Scripture. This feature takes you back in time to explore the surrounding history, culture, and customs of the ancient world.

Our prayer is that this Insight for Living Ministries Bible Companion will not only help you dig deeper into God's Word but also provide insights and application for *real* life.

BIBLICAL PARENTING

Lesson One

Discovering Your Child— and Yourself

Proverbs 22:6

THE HEART OF THE MATTER

Is anything more fulfilling (or frustrating!), more meaningful (or mysterious!), more gratifying (or grueling!), more satisfying (or surprising!) than rearing your children? What a joyful and rewarding experience it can be; at the same time, what a challenging and demanding task! Have you ever wondered if you might be going about this business of parenting all wrong? Could it be that you have never examined, in depth, what the Bible teaches about knowing and training your child? Frankly, that is where most moms and dads—believers and unbelievers alike—find themselves. If we hope to get parenting right, we must know and follow the vital truths and principles God has recorded for us in His Word. The best parenting starts with discovering who your child is. Amazingly, in the process you may also discover yourself!

DISCOVERING THE WAY

Bringing up children has to be one of the most difficult and rewarding tasks God has placed in the hands of humanity. While other creatures bring up their young purely by instinct, human beings have the faculty of reason to cloud and, eventually (hopefully!), clear the air. From the moment we meet our children, we parents ask ourselves questions that appear unanswerable: *Which brand of bottle will best deliver milk to our baby? Which method of discipline will help our child grow into maturity? How are we going to connect with our child in the hormonal-teenager years?*

Feeling pressured to answer questions like these, we often fall back on the same strategies our parents used on us. Some of these strategies can be helpful, but others may be detrimental, especially when applied to a particular child. Regardless, before we apply *any* strategy to one of our own children, we need to reflect carefully on both the strategy and the child in order to see how best to draw upon the lessons of our parents' choices and make the proper choices for our own children.

Consider your best qualities and strongest attributes, and answer the following question: What was your parents' greatest positive contribution to your becoming who you are?

_____

_____

_____

In your childhood, which quality or pattern of childrearing by your parents was the most detrimental to your view of yourself and to your ability to become a successful adult?

_____

_____

_____

_____

We've Missed What Proverbs 22:6 Teaches

Some of us have inherited a strange idea about parenting as Christians. We've received this idea from our well-intended parents, our churches, and our reading, but unfortunately, it's just not very helpful. And it's all based on a misreading of Proverbs 22:6.

Read Proverbs 22:6.

This proverb on childrearing has long been taught with a perplexing interpretation that goes something like this: "Rear your children as moral, upright, God-fearing, church-going kids. Be sure they carry Bibles to church, attend lots of Sunday school classes, and attend Christian summer camps. Enforce your rules and regulations with consistency. Make sure they learn the Ten Commandments, the Golden Rule, and several key verses of Scripture. Teach them to pray, and be sure they come to a saving knowledge of Jesus Christ. After all, they're eventually going to sow their wild oats. They'll live in rebellion for a while. Then, once they've tired of their fling with the wild side, they'll come back to the Lord . . . but only if you raised them right!"

This interpretation is not helpful, it's not very hopeful, and it's not an accurate understanding of the rich, picturesque language of the original Hebrew. This teaching focuses on a legalistic approach to childrearing when the focus should be on character development in accordance with the unique abilities and personalities of our children. If we study the Hebrew terms and how they are put together, we'll discover a very refreshing, sensible approach to childrearing that offers both hope and practical guidance.

Let's Learn What the Verse Means

Proverbs 22:6 contains only eight Hebrew words, each one packing a wealth of illustration and cultural analogy. Let's study each word in detail.

"Train Up . . ."

The Hebrew word *hanakh* means to "train up a youth" or to "dedicate." It's used only four times in the Old Testament: three times in reference to dedicating a building and once of a child, here. In Arabic, we find a very close cousin to *hanakh*; that Arabic verb pictures the ancient custom of a midwife dipping her finger into a pool of crushed dates in order to massage the palate and gums of a newborn. This encouraged the baby's sucking instinct so that nursing could begin as soon as possible. In other ancient languages, similar terms mean to "make experienced, submissive, etc. (as one does a horse by a rope in its mouth)."[1]

So, in this single term translated "train up," we have the mingled ideas of "dedicate," "mouth," and "make experienced." Also included is the picture of a horse's bridle, which subdues the horse for the purpose of directing its natural energies.

Consider the images that the Hebrew word for "train up" and its Arabic cousin evoke. What do the images have in common?

_____

_____

_____

How might these images relate to childrearing?

_____

_____

_____

"... A Child ..."

The Hebrew term *na'ar* can refer to a little child, but it also can mean a man or woman of any age still living under a parent's roof or in the care of an authority figure. The term, therefore, includes many of the "rebellious teen years." This broader definition of *child* frees us from reading this verse with an expectation of rebellion from our children. Instead, we can plan for a healthy relationship with our children, one in which we are training them and creating a taste within them for the things of God.

The Hebrew word *na'ar*, translated "child" in Proverbs 22:6, translates to similar terms such as *boy* or *youth* in other parts of Scripture. In each of the following verses, *na'ar* refers to a person in a story. Based on the clues you find in each story, estimate the approximate age of the "child."

Verse	Approximate Age
1 Samuel 4:21	
Exodus 2:6	
1 Samuel 1:22; 3:1	
Genesis 21:12	
Genesis 37:2	
Genesis 34:19	

". . . The Way He Should Go . . ."

The whole meaning of Proverbs 22:6 turns on this phrase! Many parents emphasize the word *should*, reading, "in the way he *should* go," which they consider *their* way. However, the literal Hebrew reads, "in accordance with *his* way" (the child's), or even more literally, "upon the mouth of his way." (There's *mouth* again, forming a wordplay with *hanakh*.)

All children have their own unique "way," a characteristic manner that distinguishes them from all other children, including brothers and sisters. We receive each child from the hand of God, not as a malleable lump of clay to be molded in whatever way we see fit but as a distinctive person with a destiny. We must honor God's creation of this one-of-a-kind individual by adapting our training to the child's way.

Does training up a child in his own way, as Proverbs 22:6 tells us to, mean allowing that child to do whatever he or she pleases? What Scripture verses guide your thinking here? (Hint: seek out the proverbs on discipline.)

_____

_____

_____

_____

_____

 DIGGING DEEPER
The Way

Recognizing the uniqueness of each child does not discount the reality that there are truths that apply to all people. While we as parents always desire to be sensitive to the unique needs and personalities of our children, we also want to ensure that they understand the particular, narrow road that all who claim belief in Christ should follow.

This road, or *way*, leads us to consider the early Christians, who were identified by the term "the Way" in the first century (Acts 24:14). This term comes, no doubt, from the early Christian teaching that Jesus was Himself the Way (John 14:6). With this in mind, Christian parents will see the value of pointing their children down the narrow path of following Jesus—a path paved with stones of compassion, truth, kindness, and love. We want to encourage these universal qualities in our children, no matter their particular personalities.

"... When He Is Old ..."

In this verse, the word *old* finds inspiration in the image "hair on the chin." The first wisps of hair growing on the chin of a young man show that manhood is not far away. Here, *old* doesn't mean "one foot in the grave"; it means "when he is mature." Hair begins to appear on the face of a young man at about the age of fifteen or sixteen, and likely the age of maturity for young women corresponds. In other words, as soon as young people begin to exercise their independence as adults, their parents should see the positive results of training.

What does Ecclesiastes 12:1 command?

_____

_____

_____

How does this command correspond with our broad understanding of bringing up children?

_____

_____

_____

"... Will Not Depart from It"

The Hebrew word for *depart* means simply "to turn aside." When parents help their children know themselves and follow a path, or "way," consistent with their own individual talents, interests, and temperaments, the children find themselves walking in harmony with God's plan for them as individuals. They have no need to rebel. Their contentment keeps them sensitive to the Lord's leading. Why, then, would a child reared in this manner want to depart from the way? Most would not.

However, we must remember that proverbs are not promises but principles. As such, we appreciate the truth of a proverb's direction, even if we observe exceptions here and there.

STARTING YOUR JOURNEY

Proverbs 20:11 says, "It is by his deeds that a lad distinguishes himself / If his conduct is pure and right." Your children long to be known intimately by you, and they constantly drop clues—ones that distinguish themselves—for you to notice. If we hope to adapt our training in order to cooperate with God's design of each of our children, we must first know them as individuals, accounting for their positive traits and their sinful tendencies. And that comes by careful observation, over time.

What nonphysical trait in your child stands out the most to you? This could be a talent, a temperament, an interest, a habit, a way of interacting with the world—anything. If you have more than one child, answer this question and the ones that follow for each of your children, taking into account their differences.

_____

_____

_____

_____

_____

How is this trait positive? How can your child use it constructively?

_____

_____

_____

_____

How is this trait negative? How can it negatively impact your child?

_____

_____

_____

_____

How does this trait challenge you as a parent?

_____

_____

_____

_____

In what ways does your child struggle with sin?

_____

_____

_____

_____

How can you reinforce the proper path for your particular child away from a particular temptation?

_____

_____

_____

_____

_____

When you help your children know themselves, the way that God has prepared for them will become self-evident. His ordained path will be a natural fit for the people they will become as they grow. As you adapt your childrearing to cooperate with your children's individual temperaments, interests, and abilities, you'll likely find that they have no desire to depart from the path—vocational and spiritual—that you have helped them discover. And in the process, you may even find that you've learned something about yourself—your own struggles and strengths—that can aid you in connecting more deeply with your children as you help them mark the paths of their own lives.

Lesson Two

The Bents in Your Baby
Selected Scriptures

THE HEART OF THE MATTER

One of the most frequent mistakes parents make is thinking that when they have a baby, the infant comes to them like a soft piece of clay. Most parents believe a child can be easily shaped into whatever is best for that child—and since they (the parents) believe *they* know what's best, they train their little one in the way *they* are convinced that child should go. It isn't too many years before the fight is on! As time passes, the struggle intensifies, and the battle with the child's will becomes more difficult. Conflicts abound, frustrations mount, and then—before mom and dad are ready—those inevitable teenage years arrive, introducing challenges that border the unbearable! No matter how hard parents try, the child is determined to go in a direction different from the parents' desire, and the rebellion persists. What went wrong? What's missing from this domestic equation? Why is the battle so difficult? The problem boils down to the natural "bents" in every baby.

DISCOVERING THE WAY

Nothing is easy about parenting. Anyone who believes it's effortless ignores the hard realities of guiding the growth of a complex human being. Parenting challenges us in ways we never could have predicted. These obstacles will test our minds, strain our emotions, and try our stamina. But with the challenges of parenting come deep, abiding joys. This mixture of difficulty and joy mirrors the complex reality of our children's makeup as God's good creations born with the propensity to sin.

Think back to the days before you became a parent. What expectations did you have regarding parenting? Did you think it would be easy or difficult? Joyful or strained?

_____

_____

_____

_____

How were those expectations fulfilled? Describe the greatest challenges and joys you have encountered as a parent.

_____

_____

_____

_____

A Quick Review of Where Everything Starts

No parent will be perfect. We cannot expect to get ourselves right before embarking on the journey of parenthood. This side of heaven, we will always fall short of God's design for us. And yet, we must pursue His design for our lives, knowing that when we live it out more fully ourselves, we will, in turn, be able to guide our children in the way He has laid out for His people.

 Read Proverbs 22:6.

Strong, committed, Christian parents will take into account the individuality of their children. Every child is different; therefore, every child deserves to be treated as a unique individual with particular talents and inclinations. We would do well to acknowledge these differences in our children by providing a home in which they can flourish as the people God made them to be.

Chuck Swindoll paraphrases Proverbs 22:6 this way:

> Fit the training of your child so that it is in keeping
> with his or her individual gift or bent, remembering
> the God-given abilities and characteristics they were
> born with as well as the dark side, the child's tenden-
> cies toward disobedience and rebellion, knowing
> that when that child comes to maturity he or she will
> know who they are and therefore will not turn aside
> from the training they received.

A Careful Study of Why Every Child Is a Challenge

Understanding our children as individuals requires taking into
account the particular areas in which they excel. Let's start by looking
at those good qualities—or good "bents."

 Read Psalm 139:13–16.

The psalmist laid out in wonderfully poetic language a fundamental truth that sits at the heart of our understanding of ourselves:
we are beings created by the all-powerful God. He formed every
aspect of our person, visible and invisible. Genesis 1:31 teaches us
that God called His creation of human beings "very good." This truth
should inform how we think about ourselves and, by extension, how
we think about our children. God sees each of us as His "very good"
creations—living, breathing, embodied people with particular gifts
and talents.

When we adopt such a perspective of our children, we begin to
see them in a more redemptive fashion, in spite of the sinfulness they
inherited from Adam. Our children are good gifts from God, and we
have the privilege of bringing them up in the way God would have
us to. Part of that process involves taking into account each of our
children's individual gifts and talents, recognizing those "good bents"
as part of God's "very good" creation.

Take a close look at Psalm 139:13–16. What parts of himself does the psalmist attribute to God's creation?

_____

_____

_____

_____

In verse 14, how does the psalmist describe God's work of creation?

_____

_____

_____

_____

What does this description suggest to you about the psalmist's perspective on God's creation of human beings (and of the psalmist himself)?

_____

_____

_____

_____

Were children merely collections of good traits with cute faces, parenting would be relatively simple. However, as any parent can attest, children don't come with simply good traits. They arrive with a propensity to sin as well, a propensity we might call the evil "bents."

Read Psalm 51:5 and 58:3–4.

Are children really *that* bad? Psalm 51:5 describes people as sinful from birth. Psalm 58:3–4 echoes this truth, suggesting that wickedness begins from the womb. But, *how can an infant be sinful?*

Read Romans 3:9–18. According to Romans 3:9, what percentage of the human race is "under sin"? (Some Bible versions use the word *Greeks* to denote Gentiles or non-Jews.)

_____

According to Romans 3:10–11, what percentage of the human race is righteous, understands spiritual matters, and seeks God?

_____

According to Romans 3:12, what percentage of the human race (past and present) rebels against God, does evil, and has become useless?

_____

What two powerful images do you find in Romans 3:13 that describe the extent of human depravity?

_____

_____

Christians have been debating the origin and meaning of human depravity for nearly the entire history of the church. In the fifth century AD, a monk named Pelagius proposed the idea that people are born without a sinful nature. Pelagius suggested that rather than passing on sin to us through heredity, the first man, Adam, merely set a bad example for the rest of humanity—an example we all have followed.

Augustine, a prominent church bishop, challenged Pelagius, pointing to passages such as Romans 5:17–19 that reveal a different idea. Augustine taught that people are not morally neutral but rather corrupt as a race and incapable of good unless prompted by God. Augustine's view has the weight of biblical evidence on its side. Moreover, if people are not enslaved by a sinful nature, at least a handful of the multiple-billions of people living today should be sinless. But our experience on earth tells us that's not true. So does God's Word: "There is none righteous, not even one" (Romans 3:10).

In Psalm 51:5, David wrote, "In sin my mother conceived me," which some have used to suggest that David was illegitimate or that the act of conception is sinful. Neither fits well within the context of the psalm, in which David admitted his own sinfulness, not that of his parents. He declared that he, like all people, was born as a sinful creature. Later, in Psalm 58:3, the psalmist reinforced the truth that all people are born with evil bents.

Read Romans 5:12. What brought sin into the world?

_____

Who is the "one man" originally responsible for the inherited disease of sin?

_____

According to Romans 5:17–19, what are three tragic outcomes of Adam's sin that still afflict us today?

"By the transgression of the one . . . _____

_____." (Romans 5:17)

"Through one transgression there resulted . . . _____

_____." (Romans 5:18)

"Through one man's disobedience . . . _____

_____." (Romans 5:19)

The Bible makes it clear that all human beings—even sweet little babies—have inherited a sinful nature. Beating in the chest of each and every one of our children is a strong, selfish will that leads them to do almost anything to please themselves and be happy. Children think that by having their own way, they can avoid painful experiences and sate their desires—all without negative consequences. They're convinced that they know what is best, and when faced with a moral dilemma, they will choose whatever serves them. A child's nature is to fight for immediate gratification.

STARTING YOUR JOURNEY

Our children are fallen human beings—God's good creations tainted by the evils of sin. This complex mix creates for parents what can be a difficult road to navigate. The following twofold plan can help parents succeed at producing contented children who walk steadily on the road to God's kind of success.

First, *parents need to cooperate with the good bents.* We need to look for and encourage the particular talents and gifts God has given our children. A child's good bent may be a talent in the arts or an interest in the sciences or a propensity to serve others or a willingness to sacrifice. Whatever our children's good bents may be, we parents need to provide opportunities for our children to flourish in those particular areas.

Reread Psalm 139:13–16 thinking about your children. How can you see God's design and purpose in your children's lives? Be specific.

_____

_____

_____

_____

What activities can you do with your children that will help bring to the surface their individual interests and abilities?

_____

_____

_____

_____

List the positive abilities and character qualities that you see in your children.

Abilities	Character Qualities
_____	_____
_____	_____
_____	_____
_____	_____
_____	_____

What specific things could you say or do to affirm each of your children's fundamental value to God? To you? Be creative! (You may want to consider Psalm 139 as you formulate your answer.)

_____

_____

_____

_____

Second, parents need to *counteract the evil bents*. Because our children have all been tainted by sin, they need people in their lives to point them away from the pitfalls of the sinful nature and toward productive and truly good ends. This begins with leading our children to Jesus Christ as Savior, which gives them the fundamental reason to resist temptations to sin. Each of our children—believing or not—will tend to sin in different ways. These individual acts and attitudes of rebellion require thoughtful and tailored responses from parents.

Have your children accepted Jesus Christ as Savior? If so, how does their understanding of themselves as sinners saved by grace impact their pursuit of Christ? If not (and presuming your children are of age), consider sharing the gospel with them. (To learn how to accept Jesus Christ as your Savior, please read "How to Begin a Relationship with God" on page 127 of this Bible Companion.)

Think carefully about your children. In what particular ways do they struggle with sin?

What can you do to help your children fight against and overcome their particular sin struggles?

_____

_____

_____

_____

When we determine to view our children through the balanced lens of Scripture — praising the good while curbing the evil — we give them the gifts of security and confidence. They can be secure in how God created them and confident that they can carry out His purpose as they live their lives. These invaluable gifts will give them the best opportunity to embrace what it means to be truly human — to follow after Jesus in both word and deed.

Lesson Three

Straightening Granddad's Bent

Exodus 20:4–6; 34:5–9

THE HEART OF THE MATTER

We've all heard the following words, sometimes said in affection, sometimes in disgust: "You're just like your father/mother!" In other settings, we've chided, "The acorn doesn't fall far from the tree." Are those merely throwaway clichés, or is there truth in them? We acknowledge that, being human, we are sinful people—sinners by nature, through choice and from birth. We learned in the last lesson that we were born with the same sinful nature that characterized our parents (Psalm 51:5) and that we "go astray from birth" (58:3). The prophet Isaiah correctly stated, "You have been called a rebel from birth" (Isaiah 48:8). But is the expression of our sinful condition uniquely ours, or do we inherit some of the sinful traits our parents and grandparents had? Can we trace certain acts of iniquity back to our ancestors? The answer is yes. While it may be disturbing, Scripture reveals that there are generational links to acts of iniquity. The sinful "bents" of our ancestors do not stop with their deaths. Wise are the parents who understand this, observe it in their children, and deal with it appropriately in order to bring an end to longstanding familial iniquity.

DISCOVERING THE WAY

Explorers search the land for a river's head. Geologists study deep within the earth's fissures for an earthquake's epicenter. Fire investigators sift through rubble to determine how a fire started. People of all kinds have questions about the origins of phenomena that surround them. This search extends even beyond the physical world.

Take sin, for instance. As believers, we understand that sin came into the world through Adam (Romans 5:12). But what about the *particular* tendencies toward evil that we see in ourselves and our children? We all have the potential to commit any number of sinful acts, but we have a limited number that we, as individuals, tend toward. Is there a source for those tendencies? The Bible presents us with an often overlooked answer to this all-important question.

Think about your personal struggles with specific sins. Now consider their sources. What do you believe influenced those tendencies to develop within you? (Consider specific events, people, and cultural phenomena.)

_____

_____

_____

_____

Now answer the same question in relation to the possible sources of the sinful tendencies in each of your children.

_____

_____

_____

_____

Bents in Contrast

Children are born into this world with both good and evil bents. On the good side of the ledger, they come to us with giftedness, perhaps for art, athletics, or academics. The affinity our children show for particular kinds of tasks opens a window into their makeup, into the way God created them. As parents, we have a responsibility both to look for those talents and to encourage our children in their pursuit of them. Our children will then have the potential to find lifelong satisfaction in their particular areas of giftedness.

On the other side of the ledger, we find our children's evil bents, those sinful tendencies that plague them throughout their lives. These evil bents have a common original source—Adam's fall—but they express themselves in different ways among our children. As parents, we have a responsibility to watch out for those evil bents and to counteract them in the lives of our children—first by helping lead them to salvation and then by consistently using discipline based on the Bible's identification of evil behavior.

Read Isaiah 64:6. What does this verse teach us about our condition as human beings?

_____

_____

Read Romans 3:23. What does this verse teach us about our condition as human beings?

_____

_____

Do you think these verses apply to children? Which words in these two texts give you clues to answer this question?

_____

_____

Explanation of Inherited Bents

Though most of us as Christian parents acknowledge the sinful state of our children, we haven't all given deep or careful thought to the source of our children's sinful tendencies. Where do they come from? The Bible offers one intriguing answer.

Read Exodus 20:4–6 and 34:5–9.

When God handed down the Law to His people, He began by speaking to them directly. And among His first words were ones that forewarned the people that the iniquity of a sinful idolater would pass down through three or four generations (Exodus 20:5). In other words, those who turned from the Lord, and thereby turned toward sinfulness and rebellion, could expect that the effects would carry on for generations. Sinful deeds would resonate far beyond the individual who committed them. That God repeated the phrase three other times in this period of Israel's history (Exodus 34:7; Numbers 14:18; Deuteronomy 5:9) suggests that the Creator was sending a strong message to His people who were about to inherit His gift of the Promised Land. No longer were they to live for themselves, for were they to do so, Israel would feel the effects for generations.

But what, in particular, did God say the Israelites would pass on to their children? In each case, the Lord said that the "iniquity" of the older generation would pass on to the younger. The term *iniquity* refers to a twisted mind, one that does not see the world straight. In other words, the children of rebellious Israelites would not see the world the way God had made it, but instead see it through the distorted lens passed down to them by their parents and their communities. What an obstacle for the younger generations to have to overcome!

Without the clear sight that truth and righteousness bring, these children would take on the same sinful tendencies of their parents. If dad got destructive in his anger, the kids would be more likely to lash out with fury. If mom struggled with anxiety, the kids would be more likely to worry about tomorrow. This highlights for us the destructive, cyclical nature of sin; even when we do not direct our sinful behavior toward those closest to us, it is precisely those people who suffer the most from it.

Read Ezekiel 18:14–20. What did the son see his father doing?

_____

_____

_____

_____

How did the son react to seeing all this sin?

_____

_____

_____

What was the result of the son's actions?

_____

_____

_____

If punishment is not determined by the parents' deeds (in other words, we cannot blame our parents for our sinful state), what role does the parents' sin play in the lives of their children?

_____

_____

_____

Our sins don't determine the fate of our children, but those sins certainly play a significant and influential role in the lives of our children. We can see in Scripture at least one such example.

Read Genesis 12:10–13 and 26:6–11.

Not long after Abram came into Canaan, famine struck. In search of food, Abram and his beautiful wife, Sarai, travelled to Egypt. But Abram was worried. He thought that as a man travelling alone with a woman in a strange land, he might come to harm in a dispute over his wife. So he counseled Sarai to lie and tell others she was his sister (Genesis 12:13). Many years later in the south of Canaan, Abram—by that time, Abraham—repeated the same strategy, revealing a pattern of lying in the patriarch's life (20:2).

Both of these incidents occurred before Abraham's son, Isaac, was born. But that didn't stop the sinful behavior from passing to Isaac. Canaan once again saw famine spread throughout the land, forcing Isaac and his beautiful wife, Rebekah, to travel south in search of food. While in the land of Gerar, Isaac lied about the identity of his wife for the very same reason his father had lied: to protect himself in the event that a powerful, foreign man took a liking to his wife (26:7–9).

These incidents indicate a pattern in the life of this family. *Like father, like son* appropriately describes the way the sinful behavior passed from one generation to the next. Did that make Abraham responsible for Isaac's sin? Of course not! However, Abraham clearly had an influence on his son's behavior. In the same way, parents today influence the behavior of their children.

Read 1 Samuel 2:12–17, 22–29. What were the sins of Eli's sons?

_____

_____

_____

_____

How did Eli respond to his sons when he heard about their
behavior?

_____

_____

_____

_____

What do you think Eli's age when he finally rebuked his boys
(1 Samuel 2:22) suggests about the reason they developed the
way they did?

_____

_____

_____

_____

How did God implicate Eli in the sin of his boys (2:29)?

_____

_____

_____

_____

How does this account contribute to your understanding of
generational sin?

_____

_____

_____

_____

STARTING YOUR JOURNEY

Parents cannot take ultimate responsibility for their children's sins, but parents can recognize their role in passing on certain evil bents to their children. In that recognition, should parents just throw up their hands in frustration believing they can do nothing about who their children will become? No! There are several strategies parents can adopt to help their children grow up with as few sinful bents as possible.

First, *make it your number one priority to lead your child to a saving faith in Jesus Christ.* Our children will embrace sin more fully and completely without Christ in their lives. The gift of salvation will not only save them eternally from the effects of sin, but it will give them a direction in the lifelong fight against the habit of sin here on earth.

Second, *spend time in prayer, asking for wisdom, right timing, awareness, and determination.* Often, even when we see our own sinful habits and struggles in the lives of our children, we fail to give those connections the attention they deserve. We need to spend time praying for wisdom and discernment to help us make those connections and have more gracious and helpful attitudes as we engage our kids about their sin.

What connections do you see between your own sin struggles and those of your children? Answer regarding each of your children.

_____

_____

_____

_____

_____

Can you think of particular expressions of a sinful trait in your life that may have reinforced the presence of that same trait in your children? Name a few examples.

_____

_____

_____

_____

Take a few minutes now to pray. Bring these specific issues before the Lord, ask Him to reveal other connections, and ask Him to strengthen both you and your children in the fight against these sinful tendencies.

Third, *become a faithful student of your child.* Look carefully at each of your children. They are all different. They struggle in different ways. They need encouragement in ways unique to their struggles. The better we know our children, the more likely we will be able to help them overcome their sinful tendencies.

How are your children's struggles different from one another?

_____

_____

_____

_____

In what ways are you working to discourage those behaviors?

_____

_____

_____

_____

In what ways are you working to encourage positive behaviors in place of sinful habits?

_____

_____

_____

_____

And finally, *remain consistent and fair in your discipline.* When we see our children falling into sinful behavior, we need an appropriate response that they can count on, time after time. Often, we make our best decisions outside the heat of the moment, when we are less influenced by the emotions of whatever has just gone wrong. So in a time of peace, consider each of your children's struggles and an appropriate response you will give when the time arises. When our kids have firm boundaries they can lean on, they can pursue a life of goodness with confidence, knowing just where they should and should not go.

Our responsibility as parents could not be more significant. We are building into the lives of other human beings in ways that no one else can replicate. The sheer amount of time and implicit influence that come with our roles as moms and dads carry with them the opportunity to make the most significant contributions to the lives of our children. And specifically, counteracting their sinful behaviors with consistency and wisdom is a contribution that will help not only our children but also the many lives they will touch as they grow into adulthood.

Lesson Four

Unpacking Our "Ancestral Baggage"
Genesis 25:19–21, 24–28

THE HEART OF THE MATTER

"Tell me about your parents and your family?" This question is asked by diagnostic physicians doing workups on our physical health. It's also asked by psychologists as they assist us in understanding our mental and emotional battles. The same question also needs to be asked as we consider the longstanding habits that threaten our walks with Christ. We know that we are all sinful and in need of salvation, but often, we fail to consider that we bear the *specific* "bents" of our parents, grandparents, and even great-grandparents. When we do, all of us must admit the direct link between the people we have become and the lives of those who formed our heritage—for good and for ill. In light of all this, the importance of tracing our way back through our ancestral roots should come as no surprise to those of us who desire to know our children fully. Making this journey into our pasts will help us understand why certain character traits remain so deeply embedded in our offspring and can help us break the cycle of familial sin.

DISCOVERING THE WAY

The oceans of our planet remain the single most unexplored areas on earth. While we have accumulated a variety of knowledge about sea creatures, currents, and even parts of the ocean floor, the amount that scientists don't know continues to dwarf what they do know. Why is our knowledge of the

31

sea so limited? Simply stated, it's difficult to see beneath the surface. And while we have explored beneath the surface of smaller, more manageable objects like human bodies or any number of places on land, the vast size of our oceans increases the difficulty.

Too often, the lives and motivations of our children remain as unexplored as our oceans. Though many have thought long and hard about their kids, seeing beneath the surface to what's really going on often seems as difficult as walking the ocean floor. We long to understand them, but we just don't know how. The frustration can be overwhelming, and when our children sin, the unexplained weighs even heavier on our hearts.

Take a look beneath the surface of your children. What are some possible motivations and sources for their sinful habits?

_____

_____

_____

_____

_____

A Brief Review of Our "Bents"

As parents, we're called to cultivate our children's talents, skills, and gifts. As our children grow, we should enhance those abilities with teaching on how Jesus would have us all live. We should teach them about forgiveness, compassion, kindness, and love. Much of our parenting lies on the side of encouragement—of propelling our children toward positive goals. But we also recognize that our children come to us as sinners. Therefore, a portion of our parental responsibility consists of counteracting their sinful habits. And just as our children have different gifts and talents among themselves, they have different sinful tendencies. Therefore, we must work with each of our children as individuals, enhancing their good bents and working against their evil ones.

A Case Study of "Ancestral Baggage"

Parenting makes a bit more sense when we understand that our children's sinful tendencies often have a history that goes back to before they even were born. We inherit many of our particular sin struggles from our parents and grandparents—a reality the first book of Scripture makes all too clear.

When God chose Abraham to be the father of a new nation, the Lord did not choose a perfect human being. Abraham came out of an idolatrous community in the east and travelled with his family to Canaan in response to God's direction. But Abraham's obedience to God in one area did not prevent the patriarch from faltering in other areas.

As we saw in the previous lesson, both Abraham and his son Isaac suffered from a strained relationship with the truth. Scripture records Abraham lying twice (Genesis 12:10–13; 20:2), both times before Isaac came upon the scene. But by the time Isaac had grown to adulthood, he had learned the family tendencies, evidenced by his using the same dishonest tactics for the same reasons his father had (26:7).

 Read Genesis 27:18–24.

Isaac's specific sin of lying went back to Abraham, but it didn't stop with him or even with his son. Abraham's grandson Jacob revealed himself to be up to the challenge of giving life to their particular family sin. But Jacob didn't get there alone; his mother, Rebekah, enabled him. When it came time for Isaac and Rebekah's firstborn, Esau, to claim his blessing from his aging father, Rebekah prompted their younger son, Jacob, to deceive his father and gain the blessing for himself (Genesis 27:6–13).

Rebekah's pointed actions represent one way sins pass through generations. But more often, sins are passed on in families without thought or intentionality. Even Rebekah was likely only thinking of the immediate and not of the long-term consequences of her choice to lead her boy into deception. Like we often do today, she probably chalked up the act to a single "broken egg" necessary to make the omelet. Sure, they got a little dirty in the process of lying. But the circumstances turned out as they should—at least according to Rebekah.

What was the result of Jacob's deception within their immediate family (Genesis 27:41–42)?

_____

_____

_____

_____

_____

Why do you think Jacob's act prompted such a reaction?

_____

_____

_____

_____

_____

Later, how did Jacob's act of deception influence his relationship with his father-in-law, Laban (Genesis 30:25–43)?

_____

_____

_____

_____

Interestingly, God chose a family of liars from which to birth the nation of His people and, ultimately, to birth the Savior Himself. What does this suggest to you about God?

_____

_____

_____

_____

_____

 Read Genesis 37:18–36.

The lies continued. What began with Abraham, passed on to Isaac, then to Jacob, and then to Jacob's sons, who turned on their younger brother Joseph, their father's favored son. The favoritism contributed to the brothers' ill will, as did Joseph's belief that he would one day rule them all, despite most of them being older than he. Eventually, the brothers took their opportunity to rid themselves of Joseph, selling him to a group of traders heading to Egypt, where Joseph was sold into slavery. After betraying their brother, the sons returned to their father and claimed that Joseph had been mauled by a wild animal and had died.

DIGGING DEEPER
The Growth of a Lie

We have seen the pattern of lying that followed Abraham's family through the generations. Although the sin itself—lying—continued as a constant throughout the family, the destructiveness of that sin grew in magnitude across the generations. Abraham lied to protect himself from an unwanted confrontation over his wife. Isaac copied his father, offering the same kind of lie in virtually the same situation. But then Isaac's wife joined in the lies. The propensity to lie spread, and the lies began to take place within the family between its members, rather than simply outside it.

After he left home and married Laban's daughters, Jacob deceived his father-in-law to garner a better flock for himself. The lies had not only moved within the family; they were becoming increasingly motivated by personal gain rather than by protective instinct. When the lying eventually reached Jacob's sons, they denied the truth in one of the gravest ways possible: they called someone dead who was truly alive. Their lie robbed their father of much of his joy and left him despondent for years.

What began with a simple lie from Abraham to a foreign king as a means of protection became something unwieldy, destructive, and selfish within the family God had chosen to be His people.

 Read Genesis 50:19–20.

The pattern could easily have continued with Joseph. After being sold into slavery, Jacob's son could have allowed bitterness to turn him into one of the greatest deceivers known to history. But God had

other plans. Joseph retained his trust in God, slowly rose from slave
to Egypt's second-in-command, and then found himself in a position
of power over his brothers—meting out food to them in Egypt while
their land, Canaan, struggled through famine.

Joseph could have allowed bitterness to overwhelm him when
his brothers sought his help. He could have thrown them into prison,
where they would have rotted for the rest of their days. Instead,
he saved them from starvation and, ultimately, gave God credit for
bringing them all together again. Indeed, Joseph stands as a shining
example of one who broke the chain of familial sin. He refused to
follow the path of his fathers and brothers and instead sought out a
better, more God-honoring way to live.

**In Genesis 50:19–21, Joseph repeated himself. What did he
repeat?**

_____

_____

_____

_____

**How do you think fear contributes to the continuation of familial
patterns of sin?**

_____

_____

_____

_____

How did Joseph show his brothers that he bore them no ill will? Did he rely simply on his words?

_____

_____

_____

_____

STARTING YOUR JOURNEY

We have seen the destructive pattern of sin that grows within families, distorting our relationships from what God intended. But how can we avoid falling into the trap that once captured the families of Abraham, Isaac, and Jacob? How can we deal with the ancestral baggage each of our families carries?

First, *investigate your ancestry*. We need to understand where we have come from if we expect to understand the ways that inherited sin makes itself known in our families. This means looking to the lives of our parents, grandparents, great-grandparents, and beyond for insight into their struggles with particular sins.

Second, *remember your immediate family history*. The past generations of our families don't hold all the clues about our inherited sins. Our immediate families themselves can reveal patterns of sin and unwholesomeness that have persisted. Evaluating our immediate families in this way can be difficult, but honesty about ourselves and our families is essential to moving past our areas of struggle.

Third, *take personal responsibility*. The first two steps involve evaluation; the final step involves action. We cannot just ignore what we know about the inherited sins in our families. Nor can we point the finger at someone else. If our children's sins are inherited, they implicate us as well. We need to take responsibility for our part.

When you look back into your family's history, what inherited sins do you perceive? Be specific.

_____

_____

_____

_____

_____

How have those sins carried over into your immediate family? How do each of your family members struggle with inherited sins?

_____

_____

_____

_____

_____

Think back to Joseph's response in Genesis 50:19–20. How can you and your family model that response and thereby break the chain of inherited sin?

_____

_____

_____

_____

_____

Write a prayer on the lines below. Thank God for giving you insight into your family, and ask Him to help you and each of your family members overcome the particular struggles you have in your lives.

_____

_____

_____

_____

_____

_____

_____

_____

Every family struggles with inherited sin. The first family in Israel's history didn't escape its effects. And neither will our families today. However, we need not languish in sin without recourse. We can experience growth. And we can cast off that sin which enfolds us. Take the time to reflect on the pattern of sin in Abraham's family, as well as the faith-inspired response of his great-grandson, Joseph. And let their example offer your family ways that each of you can overcome the inherited struggles you face individually and as a family.

Lesson Five

Shaping the Will with Wisdom
Selected Proverbs

 THE HEART OF THE MATTER
Being a parent is one of life's most delightful and rewarding experiences. At the same time, it can be one of life's
most exasperating and demanding challenges. Parenting
works best when we are loving and understanding in our attitudes,
consistent and calm in our reactions, and wise and mature in our
actions. *But who on earth does all of that all the time?* We're parents who
are grateful for our children, but we're still part of fallen humanity.
This means that we're often too busy and too impatient, too quick to
jump to conclusions and too extreme in our reactions. The last thing
healthy parents want is to hurt and discourage those they love so
much. Yet, standing firm is a necessary part of training, which means
our love must sometimes be "tough," and our actions must sometimes
be strong. After all, we're dealing with children who will one day have
to discipline and restrain themselves. They learn how to do that from
parents who discipline them for wrongdoing and restrain them from
defiance and rebellion. Simply put, we must learn how to shape each
child's will with wisdom.

DISCOVERING THE WAY
Good parents have a deep desire to see their children
doing good and growing in maturity. No parent with
a right attitude toward discipline enjoys reprimanding
a child. Nevertheless, discipline is an act of love, as we see in the
example of our heavenly Father, who disciplines those He loves
(Hebrews 12:7–11).

41

The word *discipline* has its roots in the Latin term *disciplina*, which refers to teaching or education. The purpose of discipline is instruction. And as any good mentor knows, discipline must be both formative and corrective. Formative discipline teaches, encourages, mentors, and inspires, while corrective discipline curbs bad behavior or replaces incorrect thinking with truth. Our focus in this lesson will primarily be on corrective discipline.

How were you corrected as a child? Describe some typical strategies your parents used.

_____

_____

_____

How do you correct your children? What strategies do you typically employ?

_____

_____

_____

Some Necessary Distinctions

Before getting into the specifics of correcting our children, let's address a few common misperceptions and draw some important boundary lines.

First, discipline and abuse are not equal. Abuse creates terror in the heart of a child. Discipline leads to an increased sense of security. Abuse degrades and demoralizes. Discipline upholds the dignity and the value of each child. Even as we support the disciplining of our children, we must also advocate for their right treatment.

Second, when we shape the lives of our children, we must take care not to go too far—we must not crush them. Children are delicate. They require care. They come to us with innocence and an inherent desire to trust us. However, when we fail to account for their unique personalities, we risk stamping out their personal strengths, leaving them open to anger and resentment.

Finally, we need to recognize the difference between normal childishness and willful defiance. Kids make mistakes . . . often. Spilling a drink, breaking a vase, forgetting to hang the coat in the right place—these are childish behaviors that take time for our children to overcome. However, at other times, our children exhibit willful defiance—deliberate, stubborn resistance. Childish behavior needs teaching and positive reinforcement. Defiance requires a firm hand in order to prepare our children for life as adults—where defiance has little benefit.

When done correctly, discipline leaves children humble, relieved, affirmed, and confident in their relationships with their parents. Think back to how you were disciplined as a child. How did you feel during and after the experience?

_____

_____

_____

As a result of your experience, do you (or do you plan to) use the same discipline strategies? Why, or why not?

_____

_____

_____

_____

_____

Practical and Workable Suggestions

The Bible makes it clear that God supports our disciplining of our children. They need to be taught, and that teaching sometimes includes correction in addition to positive guidance and encouragement. The writer to the Hebrews rooted the idea of parental discipline in the actions of God Himself (Hebrews 12:5–11). God loves those He disciplines. In the same way, we show love to our children when we take the time to discipline them. How many of us have overlooked bad behavior again and again, simply because we were fatigued? But, overlooking sinful habits in our children doesn't save us energy. Instead, it actually leads to our expending even more energy down the road when we have to deal with even bigger problems that have blossomed from the ones we failed to address in the first place.

Every parent wants to avoid the dramatic problems that come as a result of a lack of discipline in our children, but many parents simply don't know how. Let's take a look at four practical strategies parents should keep in mind as they discipline their children.

 Read Proverbs 13:24.

Many of the biggest discipline problems in our children don't appear until later in childhood. As young children, their capacity for destructive action is more limited, and far too many parents fall prey to overlooking the "small" sins of their preschoolers. Some parents get taken in by their young children's cuteness. Others struggle with fatigue or a lack of decisiveness. Still others hope against hope that the little problems will disappear on their own. But cuteness quickly fades, exhaustion doubles, confusion compounds, and problems grow. That's why the first strategy of good discipline is to *start early*. Don't wait. Overlooking the sins of our young children only yields heartbreak.

Early discipline gives both parents and children the opportunity to better survive the more difficult years ahead by setting a pattern for the entire family to draw on as the children grow. And firm boundaries that have long been established are the best defense against the vices and temptations that await our children as they cross the bridge into independent adulthood.

What does Proverbs 13:24 reveal about discipline?

_____

_____

_____

How do you think discipline communicates love to a child? How do you think a lack of discipline communicates rejection to a child?

_____

_____

_____

 Read Proverbs 29:15.

Once we've started early, we can focus on the next strategy of good discipline: *stay balanced.* Proverbs 29:15 presents two elements of good discipline: corporal punishment (the rod) and verbalized correction (reproof). We need to strike a good balance between the two. Our children need to hear what they've done wrong so they can move forward with the confidence that comes from knowing where the boundaries lie. If parents only offer quick smacks on the bottom, children can very well be left confused about what they did wrong. Words, therefore, should always accompany the rod.

Further, our words need not all be dedicated to pointing out the wrong done. We should also use our words to teach our children the beauty of God's grace—we have all fallen from the path, but God is always ready to offer forgiveness to repentant hearts.

A third discipline strategy that parents should employ addresses frequency: *be consistent*. Everyone lives under authority. Some do so willingly; others constantly fight against whatever authority God has placed in their lives. Consistency in discipline helps our children learn to live under authority, first as children and later as adults. Our consistency also helps lead our children toward authentic living. No one should have two separate lives—a public one that boasts a pristine image and a secret one riddled with selfish pursuits. Our consistency in discipline helps model for our children how to be consistent in their own lives.

Finally, *remain reasonable*. As imperfect human beings, we tend to lose our reason in the most intense moments. Often when our children stray from the path, we make rash decisions that engender exasperation in our children. However, when we remain reasonable, our children benefit from our clear thinking about who they are and the appropriate discipline we apply to what they have done.

Read Ephesians 6:4 and Colossians 3:21. What are some errors in discipline that parents make that cause their children legitimate anger, resentment, bitterness, or exasperation?

_____

_____

_____

_____

_____

What are the short-term versus long-term results of corrective discipline, according to Hebrews 12:11?

_____

_____

_____

_____

_____

If a new parent were to ask you, "What does the Bible say about discipline?" how would you respond?

_____

_____

_____

_____

_____

Using the rankings below, rate your willingness to apply corrective discipline.

> 1 — I refuse.
>
> 2 — I am very reluctant.
>
> 3 — I am indifferent.
>
> 4 — I don't like it, but I acknowledge it is important.
>
> 5 — I believe corrective discipline is crucial if my children are going to learn self-control.

Explain why you chose the ranking on the previous page.

_____

_____

_____

_____

 GETTING TO THE ROOT
Spare the Rod . . .

In most Bible versions, the Hebrew word translated "rod" refers to a wide range of wooden implements, including a thick club, a short stick, and a long pole. In Hebrew, _rod_ refers to a tool used as a cooking utensil for grinding herbs and spices such as dill and cumin (Isaiah 28:27), as a weapon (2 Samuel 23:21), and as a shepherd's staff (Psalm 23:4). Very often, the Hebrew word for _rod_ refers to a scepter (Genesis 49:10). _Rod_ also indicates an instrument of punishment for slaves (Exodus 21:20), fools (Proverbs 10:13), and sons. Depending on the context, the rod symbolizes protection, authority, and correction, and in some cases, it carries a sense of all three at once.

When used in connection with parents, the rod often addresses discipline in the broadest sense: authority, leadership, correction (Proverbs 29:15). It usually refers to corrective action, including but not limited to corporal punishment (13:24; 19:18). And sometimes, "the rod" is an expression for spanking (23:13–14), pointing to a neutral implement in the hands of an authority figure. In every such case, the rod is an instrument of love, never an outlet for parental anger. Its purpose is correction, never punishment for its own sake.

STARTING YOUR JOURNEY

In the arena of disciplining and shaping our kids' will with wisdom, parents and children can benefit from setting two significant goals. First, parents should strive *to release into the world a very responsible young adult who loves Christ.* Responsibility will not come without discipline. Second, children should strive *to become mature, Christ-honoring individuals.* Maturity comes as a result of discipline. And that result will positively impact every person our children come into contact with.

As a parent, how do you help your children grow in responsibility? Be specific.

_____

_____

_____

_____

_____

What challenges have you and your children encountered as you have sought to teach them responsibility?

_____

_____

_____

_____

_____

_____

How have you dealt with some of those challenges?

_____

_____

_____

_____

_____

Do you feel your children are mature for their ages? How has your role as parent enhanced that maturity?

_____

_____

_____

_____

As humans, we want what we want, when we want it, with no cost. However, maturity requires the ability to control our impulses and foresee the consequences of our actions. Parents have the responsibility of shaping their children into healthy adults by encouraging self-control and promoting this kind of maturity. When we do, our children will gain the capacity to enjoy helpful instruction, greater freedom, and ever-increasing blessing.

Lesson Six

Delighting in Your Children
1 Thessalonians 2:5–12

 THE HEART OF THE MATTER
We have spent quite a bit of time focusing on the
demanding challenges of rearing children: acknowledging
depravity, confronting defiance, addressing disobedience,
and dealing with rebellion. While we cannot and should not ignore
these realities, it is easy to come to the conclusion that there's nothing
but struggle when it comes to preparing our children for life on their
own. Not so! According to the psalmist, God gives each child as "a
gift"—not as a challenge. "The fruit of the womb is a reward"—not
a problem (Psalm 127:3–4). While parents need to stand firm on
issues that call for a strong hand, disciplining our children must never
eclipse delighting in them! Throughout the fabric of Scripture, God
has woven numerous statements underscoring the importance of not
only expressing but also demonstrating affirmation, encouragement,
gentleness, fun, tenderness, and affection toward our children. Let's
turn our attention to those all-important attitudes and actions that
bring joy and build esteem as we cultivate an atmosphere of harmony
and pleasure in the home.

 DISCOVERING THE WAY
We live in a world filled with negativity. Turn on the news,
and the vast majority of the stories feature violence or
loss. Take stock of your friends and family, and the difficult times in their lives will be hard to miss. Look around your own
home, and you won't be able to ignore the trials that have come upon
you. Negativity surrounds us. But, in many ways, seeing the positive

amidst the negativity requires little more than a change in perspective, a decision on our part to see the good in spite of the bad.

Acclaimed novelist Fyodor Dostoevsky once wrote, "To see only the bad is worse than seeing nothing."[1] We have to choose to see the good and the beautiful in our world. As believers who place our hope in Jesus to bring about a thoroughly good world, it makes perfect sense for us to approach any topic with a positive mind-set—one that sees God at work in the world. That includes thinking about our families.

Do you tend to see your immediate family (spouse, children) in a positive or negative light?

_____

What aspects of your behavior reveal your feelings about your family?

_____

_____

_____

Think Back:
As a Child, Was Your Home a Happy Place?

Was your childhood home a happy place? Did your parents make you feel welcome and secure? Not everyone can answer with a resounding yes. In fact, many would answer no without hesitation. A sad, largely hidden reality exists in many homes today and in the past: parents have not cherished their children. Instead, children have ended up victims of neglect. And parents have ended up "too busy" to truly engage their children and show them the attention they deserve. Can parents look to the Bible for specific guidance to address this reality? Yes!

Biblical Words That Portray a Happy Home

The Bible does not ignore parents. As one of the foundational institutions of human society, the family receives its fair share of attention in Scripture. We find at least eight unique words in the Bible that guide us in how we should interact within our families.

 Read Proverbs 3:12.

Proverbs 3:12 focuses primarily on discipline, but it also reveals something significant about the proper relationship between parents and children. When parents care enough to correct their children, they reveal their *delight* for their children. Discipline is one of the most taxing responsibilities of parenting. As a result, many parents prefer seeking out peace and solitude over taking the time for correction. The Bible, therefore, compares the parent who corrects to God Himself. The Lord never tires. He is always willing to correct His children as we slowly grow into maturity. As God does, so too does the good parent.

This proverb makes its point by playing against our expectations. Those of us who have disciplined a child understand how it saps our physical, emotional, and even spiritual energy. So, the proverb's insertion of delight may initially surprise the reader. When the topic of discipline arises, we except drudgery, not delight. The surprise, then, enhances the effect of the proverb.

Why does God reprove people, according to Proverbs 3:12?

_____

_____

_____

_____

Why do you think this proverb associates love with the practice of discipline?

_____

_____

_____

_____

_____

 Read Hebrews 12:5–6.

This passage from Hebrews quotes the verse that we just examined from Proverbs. However, because it was written in Greek centuries after the book of Proverbs, Hebrews 12:5–6 provides us with an additional word that informs our understanding of the proper relationship between parents and children: _receives._

Paradechomai, the Greek word the writer to the Hebrews used for "receives," occurs elsewhere in the New Testament in ways that further enhance our understanding of the term. Mark recorded Jesus using _paradechomai_ in His explanation of the parable of the sower. When the seed falls on good soil, "they hear the word and _accept_ it" (Mark 4:20, emphasis added). Luke used the term in Acts to describe the scene in which Paul and Barnabas arrived in Jerusalem for the council, noting "they were _received_ by the church and the apostles and the elders" (Acts 15:4, emphasis added). We see in these passages the sense of welcoming that comes when hearing something we appreciate or meeting someone we love. Therefore, when the Lord "scourges every son whom He _receives_" (Hebrews 12:6, emphasis added), we get the sense of God welcoming His children to Himself. As God does, so too does the good parent.

The word used by the writer to the Hebrews, *paradechomai*, occurs in other scriptural contexts. Jot down a few notes on the meaning of the terms translated from *paradechomai* in each of the following passages, paying particular attention to how those meanings enhance your understanding of the parent-child relationship.

Accept in Acts 16:21

Accept in Acts 22:18

Receive in 1 Timothy 5:19

  Read Ephesians 6:4.

In Ephesians 6:4, we find two additional key terms for understanding our responsibility to our children: *bring them up* and *instruction*. Paul used the first term just a few sentences earlier in Ephesians 5:29, where we find it translated "nourish." *Bring them up*, then, indicates that parents are responsible for sustaining, strengthening, and building up their children so they might grow into the people God has made them to be. Further, Paul wrote that parents need to bring up their children in the *instruction* of the Lord. The idea behind the word *instruction* involves more than just giving the children information. The King James Version translates this term in Ephesians 6:4 as "admonition," which helps us see a quality of warning in the instruction. In other words, parents are to warn their children away from certain kinds of thinking and behavior, pointing them instead toward the things of God.

Scan 1 Corinthians 10:1–11. Paul used the same Greek word for "instruction" in verse 11 as he did in Ephesians 6:4. In what concrete ways did the Corinthians receive instruction, according to this passage?

_____

_____

_____

_____

How does the admonition in 1 Corinthians 10 impact your understanding of _instruction_ in a parenting context?

_____

_____

_____

 Read 1 Thessalonians 2:5–11.

First Thessalonians 2 includes four more terms that can enlighten parents: _tenderly cares, exhorting, encouraging,_ and _imploring._ Paul used the first of these, _tenderly cares,_ to describe the way a nursing mother cherishes her infant child. We might insert the word _cherish_ as a synonym. God calls parents to cherish their children. Our love should overflow as we bring up these young gifts God has placed in our charge.

Not only do we need to cherish our children, we need to _exhort, encourage,_ and _implore_ them. When we _exhort_ our children, we urge them on toward good, pointing the way forward for them in a congenial fashion. _Encouragement_ is a more familiar term today and involves cheering up our children or consoling them when they are down. Finally, we *implore* our children when we affirm them and look for ways to help them accomplish the tasks before them. This requires parents to have a perspective that looks for opportunities to offer their children positive reinforcement rather than tear them down.

Tenderly caring for, exhorting, encouraging, and imploring our children can be a challenging road for us as parents—one that requires patience on our part. Treating our children in this way is easier when we remember that they have come to us from the hand of God. We have the privilege of raising these gifts of the Creator and helping them have the fulfilling lives God has planned for them.

Read Proverbs 12:25. What direction does this verse offer?

_____

_____

_____

Think about the ways your kids struggle with anxiety and other negative emotions. What kinds of *tender care, encouragement, exhortation,* or *imploring* could you give them for their specific struggles?

_____

_____

_____

STARTING YOUR JOURNEY

As parents, we should make it a point to spend ample time with our children. They need our attention. They need our presence. They need us to engage them where they are, to enter their world in the same way that God enters ours. In a busy world full of enticement, we parents need to focus more on the needs and desires of our children, incorporating those needs and desires into how we spend our time. This can be an incredibly difficult task for parents who already have more tasks on their to-do lists than they will ever get to. However, time spent with our children is vital to their health and welfare.

How do you feel about the time you spend with your children? Is it enough? Too much? Why do you think you feel this way?

_____

_____

_____

_____

As a caring parent, you, no doubt, want to spend time with your kids. Consider the eight words we have examined in this chapter. Record a specific action you could employ toward your children to represent each of the eight qualities.

Delight (Proverbs 3:12)

_____

_____

_____

Receive (Hebrews 12:6)

_____

_____

_____

Bring Them Up or *Nourish* (Ephesians 6:4)

_____

_____

_____

Instruction (Ephesians 6:4)

_____

_____

_____

Tenderly Care or *Cherish* (1 Thessalonians 2:7)

_____

_____

_____

Exhort (1 Thessalonians 2:11)

_____

_____

_____

Encourage (1 Thessalonians 2:11)

_____

_____

_____

Implore or *Affirm* (1 Thessalonians 2:11)

_____

_____

_____

What do you think is your greatest challenge to being positive and affirming with your children?

_____

_____

_____

What do you think you need to change in order to bring affirmation into your home more easily?

_____

_____

_____

_____

_____

_____

God wants us to discipline our children, to help them curb the nasty habits that their desire for sin breeds in them. However, life is not just, or even primarily, about stamping out the negative. It's also about offering a positive vision of life and godliness to our children. God wants us to be our children's greatest encouragers, as well as the ones who keep them in line. Keeping this tension can be extremely difficult for a parent . . . yet our calling it remains.

Lesson Seven

Delightful Memories Your Children Won't Forget

Psalm 127:3–128:6

THE HEART OF THE MATTER

In our thinking about the home and especially our children, we have gone back to our roots. We have thought about how God forms each person in the womb. We have discovered there are both "good bents" and "evil bents" deep within each of us. This discovery led us to realize that, as parents, our duties include cultivating those God-given interests and capabilities in our children — but not to the exclusion of dealing with disobedience, rebellion, and defiance. Next, we examined the huge responsibility of shaping each child's strong will with wisdom. Then, knowing that rearing children is much more than discipline, we turned our attention to *delighting* in our children. Due to the breadth of that last subject, we'll explore it more in this lesson. Having learned some key words in the Bible that pertain to delighting in our offspring, we now need to think about some practical ways we can do just that. As you consider these, remember: your children won't forget the occasions you make to take joy in them. Delightful memories last forever.

DISCOVERING THE WAY

We all yearn to have a little fun now and then. And yet, the busyness of our family lives — taken up with work, school, and activities — often drains away the fun. We forget fun, thinking it inessential or frivolous. And in a world of serious problems and difficult trials, we ask ourselves, "Should we really be spending our valuable time having fun?" Questions about how to best spend time plague every family. In this lesson, we'll see the importance of carving out time for positive and enjoyable experiences with the people closest to us.

Do you feel that fun and enjoyment should be a priority in the family? Why, or why not?

_____

_____

_____

_____

_____

In what ways do you and your family have fun together?

_____

_____

_____

_____

The Family: A Museum of Memories

To help us understand the importance of making delight a priority, let's consider the image of a museum, a building which holds precious treasures from the past. Within its halls, long-past events live on. Behind its doors, opportunities to revisit the past with thoughtfulness and affection abound. In the same way, we hope our children's memories hold precious moments they can look back on with fondness and joy. As they revisit those delightful times, their sense of belonging and being loved will only deepen.

The Memories: Attitudes and Activities That Say, "You're Important"

God gives us pointed and clear direction regarding the task of building up our families by communicating to them their value. Let's look to Scripture to find the attitudes and actions we can put into practice to make our children feel significant.

 Read Psalm 127:1–128:6.

Children know their importance when parents *acknowledge that their children are gifts and rewards*. The mundane can burden even the best of parents, leading them to lump their children in with the difficulties they face in life. However, God did not create children to be obstacles to our happiness. And God does not view them as burdens. Rather, the Lord tells us through the psalmist that He has made children to be the opposite of burdens: gifts and rewards (Psalm 127:3). Will there be difficult times with our children? Certainly. But when we view those times through the lens of our children being gifts and rewards, we can more easily see the Lord at work in them and in us.

The word translated "gift" in Psalm 127:3 carries with it the idea of an inheritance. When parents hand down an inheritance, what responsibility do the children carry regarding that inheritance? How does an inheritance impact a child's life?

_____

_____

_____

What do you think it means to consider our children as an inheritance from the Lord?

_____

_____

_____

Children also know their significance when parents *realize that each child is like an arrow*. The psalmist employs the image of an arrow "in the hand of a warrior" to describe the way that parents have the unique privilege of guiding the lives of their little "gifts" from God (Psalm 127:4). This task requires great care and skill on behalf of the parents. Their good guidance not only benefits their children by directing them to their proper destinations; it also increases their understanding of their own significance. When parents devote time and energy to aiming their little "arrows," children see ever more clearly their true significance, not just in the eyes of their parents but also in the eyes of God.

Reflect on the metaphor offered in Psalm 127:4. What skills would a warrior with arrows in hand need to possess?

_____

_____

_____

_____

How do you think those skills might apply to parents attempting to guide their children toward appropriate destinations?

_____

_____

_____

_____

_____

Third, children feel significant when their parents *understand that happiness and joy accompany the presence of children in the home.* Many parents feel tempted to treat children as burdens. However, as gifts from God who need our guidance, children present a wonderful opportunity for happiness and joy to extend throughout the home. When that occurs, children notice. Parents who take joy in their children give them important gifts, such as confidence and security. From that strong foundation, children have the potential to face up to all manner of challenges that will come their way. Further, parents' extending joy and happiness to their children mirrors the way God treats His children. As God does for us, so we should do for our children.

Read Psalm 149:4. What does it reveal about God?

_____

_____

_____

_____

_____

What do you think parents communicate to their children by taking joy in them? Explain your answer.

_____

_____

_____

_____

_____

DOORWAY TO HISTORY
Family in Community

Increasingly, our modern world encourages us to isolate ourselves from our broader communities. As a result, families are less connected to one another than ever. And while some family members remain united to one another, they often exist as lonely islands far from the mainland of the rest of the community.

Psalm 127:5, which recognizes the blessing of families and children, outlines the implicit connection that has historically existed within families as well as between individual families and the broader community. The psalmist pictured a quiver full of children speaking on their father's behalf in the city gate, *defending their father* against enemies. The commitment to family is unmistakable. Further, because these children speak for their father *in the public square*—ancient city gates were public meeting places—we see a connection to their community borne out of their connection to their family. Just as they serve their father by defending him, they serve their community by engaging others and staying committed to a strong home life.

In the ancient world, the children stayed connected to their families. And as children spoke on their parents' behalf in the midst of the public, they brought honor to those families while also strengthening their communities.

The Investment: What Children Long to Remember

What do children want most? This is a question that parents don't often ask themselves, leading to missed opportunities in their homes. Four things come to mind for which all children long.

First, children *long to remember that their parents made time for them.* Time is crucial—a fact parents acknowledge when it relates to work and other "grown-up" issues but often forget when it comes to their children who are always present. Nonetheless, our children need our time. They yearn for it.

Right now, what memories will your children have of the time you spent with them? How can you give them better memories?

_____

_____

Second, children *long to remember how much their parents valued them.* We must all admit that we would love to feel valued by the most important people in our lives. This desire in our kids is not unique to them.

What particular actions do you do to communicate the way you value your children?

_____

_____

Third, children *long to remember how much mom and dad loved each other.* Kids may scrunch up their faces when mom and dad show each other affection, but children really do want to know that their parents love each other deeply. Love, at its essence, is commitment. And rock-solid commitment breeds a sense of security that helps children thrive.

In what ways does your relationship with your spouse assure your children that you are committed to the family?

_____

_____

_____

_____

And fourth, children _long to remember the authentic life of faith._ Children do not take to hypocrisy—no one does really. But it can be especially damaging for a child to grow up in an environment where his or her parents act one way in public and completely different in private. The damage could be so great as to even impact the child's faith. No parent sets out to be the reason a child walks away from God. But a life of spiritual hypocrisy widens that path for our children.

Take a moment to be honest with yourself about the differences between your public and private lives. On the lines below, write a prayer asking God to help you avoid hypocrisy.

_____

_____

_____

_____

STARTING YOUR JOURNEY

We've seen what Scripture says about delighting in our children, but how can we make it a reality in our homes? Where do we start? Let's look at three pieces of advice that apply to all parents and children.

First, _delight in lingering around them._ Simply being around our children will bring a joy and excitement that will transcend so many of the difficulties they face. Not only that, spending time with our children—and enjoying it—will provide opportunities for the following two pieces of advice.

Second, *delight in listening to them.* We often hear ourselves telling our children to listen—a vital skill to help them live well in this world. However, just because we're adults doesn't mean we can forego listening ourselves! We can learn so much about our children by simply giving them opportunities to speak to us . . . and by taking them seriously when they do. They will remember our attentiveness to their concerns, even as the specifics fade into the past.

And finally, *delight in laughing with them.* From their youngest days, our children thrive on our laughter. Parents who retain a sense of humor, even when life hits in the most difficult ways, offer their children a gift that will help them live in this world and cope with the difficulties that come their way. When we don't laugh, we cut off for our children one significant avenue of making good memories.

Do you make a point of spending time with each of your children, devoting focused periods just to them? If so, when? If not, what prevents it?

_____

_____

_____

_____

What do you enjoy most about lingering, listening, and laughing with your children?

_____

_____

_____

_____

What is your greatest struggle in implementing these pieces of advice into your family's daily life?

_____

_____

_____

_____

How do you think you can better implement these three pieces of advice into your family life? Be specific.

_____

_____

_____

_____

❦

When it comes to delighting in our children, we need to remember that, at the heart of things, we're really talking about cultivating relationships with them. All too often, daily tasks get the best of our time, and our children get shuffled to the corners of our schedules. But our children's value as creations of God warrants not just our time but the best that we have to offer. Therefore, delight in your children. Give them memories they'll want to remember forever. See them as the marvelous people God has made them to be, and watch them flourish under your attentive care.

Lesson Eight

When the Fun Stops for Parents
1 Samuel 15:22–23; Luke 15:11–24

THE HEART OF THE MATTER

Every family has headaches and heartaches. Because human depravity runs deep, it is impossible to rear our children from infancy to independence without encountering times that call for straight talk and tough love. While we love our children no matter what, parents cannot escape those occasions when wills clash, rebellion reaches an impasse, and things get downright impossible. For any number of reasons, some adolescents and young adults who still live at home reach a place where they simply refuse to obey their parents. All attempts to restore harmony prove futile. And the result? Harsh words and ugly reactions as parents stand their ground and sons and daughters stubbornly refuse to back down. We pray, but nothing changes. We reason, but it's a dead-end street. We apply different measures of discipline, but things only get worse. And the realization that our other children are being neglected—or at least negatively influenced—as we spend all our energy dealing with the rebel compounds the struggle.

This is when the fun stops for parents.

DISCOVERING THE WAY

While reading the Bible to his young son, a father came to the story of Sodom and Gomorrah. "The man named Lot was warned to take his wife and flee out the city," the father read, "but his wife looked back and was turned to salt."

The little tyke asked, "What happened to the flea?"

Do you remember those days? The ones when your children were innocent, curious, and funny? How great it would be if our children could stay young and worry only about fleas! But children never stay young. They grow up. They lose their innocence. And sometimes they become curious about things better left alone. Like Lot's wife, they rebel and suffer terrible consequences, and there's nothing funny about it.

So, what are parents to do when children defy authority, unreasonably determine to go their own way, and walk the path of sin? What are parents to do when a prodigal causes pain to the family?

Look up the word *rebellion* in a dictionary and paraphrase its definition.

_____

_____

_____

How would you answer the question posed in the paragraph above: "What are parents to do?"

_____

_____

_____

An Analysis: Rebellion

In his influential essay, *The Rebel*, French philosopher, novelist, and playwright Albert Camus asked: "What is a rebel?" Camus, a rebel himself, offered a straightforward answer: "A man who says no, but whose refusal does not imply a renunciation. He is also a man who says yes, from the moment he makes his first gesture of rebellion."[1]

To say no to authority or tradition is to say yes to anarchy and
revolution, whether in civilization at large or in the home. In this
no/yes decision, rebellion either blooms full flower or withers on the
vine.

For King Saul, the decision was easy . . . and tragic.

 Read 1 Samuel 15:22–23.

Saul was a nobody who became a somebody. He wasn't born
to power and privilege; he was picked. Plucked out of all possible candidates to wear Israel's crown, Saul was chosen by God
(1 Samuel 9:15–17, 21; 15:17). But this nobody from the tiny tribe
of Benjamin had two major character flaws: impulsiveness and pride.
His impulsiveness almost led to the execution of his son, Jonathan
(14:24–45). Saul's pride led to his expulsion as king.

**Through the prophet Samuel, what did God command Saul to do
in 1 Samuel 15:1–3?**

What did Saul actually do, according to 1 Samuel 15:9–21?

Rebellion is an act of defiance toward authority and an unbending
determination to go one's own way, regardless of counsel or instruction. To use a military term, rebellion is *insubordination.*

In what does the Lord delight, according to 1 Samuel 15:22?

_____

_____

_____

Saul's disobedience resulted in a scathing indictment by the prophet Samuel, who accused Saul of "rebellion" and "insubordination" and likened those acts to "divination" and "idolatry" (1 Samuel 15:23). *Divination* is a general term for the practice of the dark arts of the occult (Deuteronomy 18:10–11). *Idolatry* is a specific term for the worship of anything or anyone other than God. Rebellion is akin to divination because rebellion comes from the demonic overlord, Satan. And insubordination is akin to idolatry because insubordination is bound up in the heart of those who presume lordship over their own lives.

Because Saul rejected the Lord's rule over his life, the Lord rejected Saul's rule over the people (1 Samuel 15:23).

A Story: A Rebellious Son

Saul's story is that of a nobody who became a somebody, but because of rebellion, the somebody was dethroned. The parable of the prodigal son is the story of a somebody who became a nobody. His rebellion led to a life of degradation.

 Read Luke 15:11–24.

"Foolishness is bound up in the heart of a child," Proverbs 22:15 warns. Foolishness may lie dormant, hidden behind innocence, but discerning parents spy its peek-a-boo play as their children grow. Rebellion is no different. In Jesus's story of the prodigal son, the father must have seen streaks of stubborn independence in his son years before the young man asked for his inheritance (Luke 15:12).

Traditionally, a father's estate was divided either at his retirement or his death. But the young man in Jesus's story didn't want to wait that long. The son longed to shake the country dust from his feet and walk city streets, so he demanded his share of his inheritance. And in accordance with the Law, the father gave his younger son one-third of the estate, while the older son received a "double portion" or two-thirds (Deuteronomy 21:15–17).

How did the father respond to his younger son's demand for money, according to Luke 15:12?

_____

_____

_____

_____

How could the father have chosen to respond to his son's rebellion, according to Deuteronomy 21:18–21?

_____

_____

_____

_____

How did the father's response demonstrate both grace and discipline?

_____

_____

_____

_____

The young man, upon filling his pockets with money, didn't immediately bolt for the door (Luke 15:13). He stayed home a few days, perhaps packing his bags and making his traveling plans. We can imagine, over the course of those days, the boy's father trying one last time to dissuade his rebellious son from running to his own ruin.

Refusing to heed his father's pleas, the young man "left for a distant country . . . [and] there, undisciplined and dissipated, he wasted everything he had" (15:13 MSG). Far from the eyes of his father, in a pagan land, the prodigal squandered his riches on "loose living"—experimenting with and experiencing all that was forbidden by God's Law and dad's rules, including visits to the red-light district (15:30).

But when a recession—"a severe famine"—hit, the prodigal's funds ran dry. He found his pockets empty and his credit denied (15:14). Destitute, the young man became desperate. His appetite to fill his stomach replaced his appetite to fulfill his sexual fantasies, and he took a job slopping pigs. So hungry was he that he would have rooted in the muck to eat the same corncobs used to feed the pigs (15:15–16).

Based on their knowledge of Deuteronomy 14:8, what would the average Jews of Jesus's day have thought about the young man in the pigsty?

_____

_____

_____

_____

_____

_____

Do you know someone who is living or has lived a "pigsty" life? If so, what led to this situation, and how does it relate to our study of rebellion within the family?

_____

_____

_____

_____

Who knows how long the prodigal's temporary insanity lasted, but one day, while standing knee-deep in the muck and mire of his pigsty, "he came to his senses" (Luke 15:17). There, among the stench of excrement and rotten food, the prodigal saw the rottenness of his rebellious soul. Lower than the pigs, the boy repented and determined to return to his father . . . not as a son but as a servant (15:17–19).

The parable of the prodigal son is really the parable of the forgiving father. We focus on the prodigal's rebellion, but he focused on his father's character. The young man said he would return to his father, whom the son believed would at least take him back as a hired hand. "So he got up" out of the slop yard and went home (15:20). He didn't even bother to hose off.

What the prodigal didn't know was that the whole time he was wasting his life, his father was waiting for his son's return. Every day for months, perhaps years, the young man's father rose early and watched the road, hoping to see the familiar figure of his son. What the father didn't know was that on a day that promised no more joy than any other day, his heart would near burst with joy abundant. Looking down the road, as he had countless days before, the father saw his boy. Before the son's mud-crusted legs could reach the house, the father ran, embraced, and lavished kisses on his son. So overjoyed was the father and so passionate his kisses, the prodigal barely blurted out his confession. The father heard not a word. The forgiving father ordered his servants to prepare a banquet as he welcomed the once rebellious boy back into the family as his son, not as a servant (Luke 15:20–24).

STARTING YOUR JOURNEY

Could there be a heartache more grievous to parents than that of a rebellious child? Prodigals bring pain, and most families have at least one. So how should you respond to the rebels in your family? The story of Saul and the parable of the prodigal provide four lessons.

Lesson 1: *No rebel can be allowed to ruin a home.* No matter how loved, gifted, or valued our rebellious children are, their unreasonable, unruly, and unresponsive rebellion must never be tolerated.

Lesson 2: *If the rebellion necessitates a separation, then so be it.* Don't let your emotions dictate your decisions when dealing with rebellious older sons or daughters. And as difficult as it may be to send a child from your home, such a separation just might save that child and your home from further heartache.

Lesson 3: *Let go of your child and release him or her to the consequences.* Don't cling to your rebellious children, and don't rescue them from the consequences of rebellion. Rebels rarely respond to reason, but they often respond to reality—the stone-cold bottom of the pit.

Lesson 4: *When true repentance occurs, let grace abound.* The prodigal's father is the preeminent example of such grace because he represents the character of our heavenly Father. All of us are rebels at heart, having spurned God and picked our own paths. But through Christ, we can come back to the Father and find forgiveness.

Consider a time when rebellion characterized your life in some way. What were the consequences?

_____

_____

_____

_____

_____

How did you respond to the reality of those consequences?

_____

_____

_____

_____

Does rebellion characterize one of your children, or do you know someone else currently dealing with a rebellious child? If so, what is the nature of that rebellion, and what consequences have come as a result?

_____

_____

_____

_____

_____

_____

How has that child responded to the reality of those consequences?

_____

_____

_____

_____

The root of rebellion is pride, and the fruit of rebellion is punishment. We've seen this in the life of an adult who should have known better—Saul. And we've seen it in the life of a young man who couldn't learn any other way—the prodigal. You might have even experienced this in your own life.

Giving over your rebellious child to the furies of reality very well may be the most difficult decision you'll ever make, but as John White observed, you might not have any choice:

> God's dealings with his people form a pattern for
> Christian parents. Like him we may eventually have
> to allow our persistently rebellious children to harvest
> the consequences of their willfulness. The time can
> come when we have to withdraw all support from
> them and oblige them, because of their own decisions,
> to leave home.[2]

This has always been true, and it has always caused pain. But as C. S. Lewis wrote: "[Pain] plants the flag of truth within the fortress of a rebel soul."[3] Such pain may be the very grace of God to transform the rebel soul into a redeemed and reconciled soul.

Lesson Nine

Resolving Those
Parent-Child Conflicts
Matthew 5:23–24; 18:21–35

 THE HEART OF THE MATTER
Conflicts are inevitable in every family. And learning to
resolve them is of vital importance. Sometimes parents
create the conflict. Often busy and preoccupied, moms
and dads react with impatience and irritability. Their words and
actions wound their sons and daughters, leaving scars that don't
go away. Children commonly offend their parents as well by acting
selfishly, responding angrily, and blurting out thoughtless words that
hurt their parents. Such behavior also results in lingering wounds that
fester over the years. Unless dealt with appropriately, conflicts lead to
permanent breakdowns in our relationships that time alone cannot
heal. How many families have grown apart due to bitter silence? How
many wrongs have been swept aside, leaving unmentioned family
secrets to linger? If we wish to cultivate healthy relationships, especially with our children, reconciliation is essential. But . . . *how?*

 DISCOVERING THE WAY
Every state, region, and country has its own colloquial-
isms—those colorful sayings that capture truth in unique
ways. Texans are particularly known for their one-line
zingers. When commenting on the heat, a Texan might say: "It'll melt
your butter and bake your biscuits." When referring to someone who
speaks before thinking: "His mouth was awake while his brain was
still asleep." Or when speaking to someone who needs to ask forgiveness: "The easiest way to eat crow is while it's still warm. The colder it
gets, the harder it is to swaller." [1]

Yes, crow doesn't taste good, and it's hard to get down your gullet, hot or cold. But it's easier to swallow than the gall of resentment. Unless its members swallow their pride and forgive offenses, a family—parents, children, or otherwise—cannot function as the Lord intends. To put it another way: the oilcan of forgiveness should ever be at hand, for forgiveness is the lubricant that keeps family friction from destroying family harmony.

Recount a time when a member of your family hurt you deeply. If you can, consider specifically a time when your child hurt you.

_____

_____

_____

_____

_____

Recount a time when you hurt a member of your family deeply. If you can, consider specifically a time when you hurt your child.

_____

_____

_____

_____

_____

An Important Word We Need to Define

"Forgiveness is love," Os Guinness wrote, "and like love it may be costly. 'One forgives to the degree that one loves,' said La Rochefoucauld. Without love, forgiveness would be pointless sentiment; without forgiveness, love would be forlorn yearning."[2]

Webster defines *forgive* as: "to give up resentment . . . [and] to cease to feel resentment against (an offender)." [3] What would you add to Webster's definition?

_____

_____

_____

_____

_____

Read the following passages, and explain what each teaches you about a forgiving spirit.

Proverbs 24:17

_____

_____

_____

Luke 6:35

_____

_____

_____

Romans 12:14–21

_____

_____

_____

In your experience, is this kind of forgiving spirit easier or harder to come by between parents and children? Why?

_____

_____

_____

_____

_____

Two Major Issues We Must Address

Resentment is a two-way street; so is forgiveness. We can control only what *we* think, feel, and do, not what anyone else does. Therefore, we'll look at resentment and forgiveness from our end of the block. From where we stand, two questions need addressing. First, *what do we do when others feel resentment toward us because we have offended them?* Second, *what do we do when we feel resentment toward others because they have offended us?*

 Read Matthew 5:23–24.

Let's deal with the first question first: *what do we do when others feel resentment toward us because we have offended them?*

The broad context of Matthew 5 deals with the relationship between Old Testament Law and righteousness. The immediate context (Matthew 5:20–26) deals with the sixth commandment in Exodus 20:13, the prohibition against murder. Jesus's point? Righteousness isn't merely measured by one's obedience to the letter of the Law; it is also measured by one's inward conformity to the spirit of the Law. We must abstain from murder, *and* we must rid ourselves of anger (Matthew 5:22). Verses 23 and 24 of Matthew 5 serve as an illustration of how seriously God takes not just the act of obedience but the heart behind it.

What verbs did Jesus use in Matthew 5:24?

_____

_____

_____

What is significant about the order of those verbs?

_____

_____

_____

Before Jesus's sacrifice on the cross, reconciliation between a sinful humanity and a holy God was accomplished through animal sacrifice, presented to the Lord at the altar in the temple on Yom Kippur, the Day of Atonement. When Jesus told offenders to leave their sacrifices before the altar and make amends with the offended, He was instructing, in that particular case, that reconciliation with others should take precedence over reconciliation with God.

Now, read Matthew 5:23–24 again and summarize it in modern-day language.

_____

_____

_____

How can you apply this interpretation to your relationships with your children?

_____

_____

_____

Read Matthew 18:21–35.

Now let's deal with the second question: *what do we do when we feel resentment toward others because they have offended us?*

The context of Matthew 18 concerns Jesus's teaching on the attitude required of all disciples. Humility is essential:

1. For entrance into God's kingdom
   (Matthew 18:2–3)

2. For greatness in God's kingdom (18:4)

3. To prevent offenses among God's people
   (18:5–10)

4. To administer appropriate discipline in the church
   (18:12–20)

5. To forgive others who have offended us
   (18:21–35)

Jesus's teaching on resolving conflict in Matthew 18:12–20 stuck in Peter's mind like a splinter. Peter understood that the measure of righteousness was humility, practiced through forgiveness. He also knew the Pharisees taught that one must forgive an offender twice, and if a Pharisee was especially righteous, he would forgive up to three times. But because Jesus taught that the righteousness of His disciples must exceed that of the Pharisees (5:20), Peter asked whether seven times (doubling the Pharisees' righteousness and adding one for good measure) would suffice (18:21).

Jesus's answer? "Seven! Hardly. Try seventy times seven" (18:22 MSG). Jesus wasn't teaching a math lesson, as if His disciples were to forgive only 490 times. He was using an ancient idiom to demonstrate that His disciples were to forgive offenses innumerable times. Thus, Jesus taught that His disciples' righteousness was measured by their forgiving offenses, regardless the number of times those offenses were committed. To drive His point home, Jesus told the parable of the wicked servant who, though forgiven an unfor-givable debt, did not forgive his fellow servant a forgivable debt (Matthew 18:23–35).

Who do the king and lord represent in the parable?

_____

_____

_____

Who does the first indebted servant represent?

_____

_____

_____

Jesus's parable refers to an impossibly high amount of money that the servant owed the king—"ten thousand talents" (Matthew 18:24). In that day, one talent equaled fifteen years' wages, making the servant's indebtedness an amount he could have never paid.

When the indebted servant came to the king after the threat of being thrown into prison (18:25–26), what did the king feel and do for his servant, according to verse 27?

_____

_____

_____

Who does the second indebted servant represent?

_____

_____

_____

What did the forgiven servant demand of the second servant? And what did the forgiven servant do to the other?

_____

_____

_____

When the king heard what the first, forgiven servant did to the second servant, what did the king do?

_____

_____

_____

How often does God forgive us, even for the same sin?

_____

What does God's compassionate willingness to forgive your sin teach you about forgiving those who sin against you?

_____

_____

_____

Have you applied Jesus's teaching in this parable to your children? If so, how? If not, why not?

_____

_____

_____

_____

_____

GETTING TO THE ROOT
A Tortured Interpretation

Jesus concluded His teaching about humility and forgiveness with a warning: "My heavenly Father will also [hand you over to the torturers], if each of you does not forgive his brother from your heart" (Matthew 18:35). Many have interpreted Jesus's words as an indication that Christians can lose salvation. Nothing could be further from the truth. Jesus made clear in John 10:27–30 that no one and nothing can snatch out of His hands those who belong to Him. But if we can't lose our salvation, what did Jesus mean?

Torturers in this passage is the Greek word *basanistes*, a term also found in extra-biblical literature to refer to prison guards who torture prisoners to elicit information or payment of debt.[4]

Practically, Jesus's use of *basanistes* indicates that our failure to forgive leads to the cruel and unrelenting torture of bitterness—a caustic acid that eats away at our relationship with the Lord and our relationships with others. The gall of resentment, hatred, and anger will stew within and poison us. Unless we decide to humble ourselves and forgive the wrongs done to us, we'll remain prisoners in a torture chamber of our own making, enduring the never-ending drip of venomous hatred.

STARTING YOUR JOURNEY

Whether we've hurt or been hurt, the right response requires this awareness: *it's my move.*

If you've offended one of your family members, it's your move to seek forgiveness and reconciliation. You don't need to keep praying about it; you need to just do it. Drop whatever you're doing and ask for forgiveness today!

Think back on that time when you hurt someone in your family (your answer on page 82). What have you done to make that wrong right—to restore harmony in your relationship?

_____

_____

_____

_____

_____

If you haven't sought forgiveness and reconciliation, you haven't done enough. Will you commit to getting in touch with that family member and asking for forgiveness? If so, sign the following contract.

> I, _____,
> resolve to swallow my pride and, with God's grace,
> seek the forgiveness of _____
> _____, in order to restore harmony in
> our relationship. I will offer no excuses, justifica-
> tions, or rationalizations for my hurtful behavior
> and/or words but will shoulder the blame for the
> breach in our relationship. I accept that it may take
> time for _____
> to accept my apology. I also accept the fact that my
> attempts at reconciliation may be rejected. If this
> happens, I will not cast aspersions, hold grudges,
> or speak evil against _____.
> Rather, I will commit to sustaining him or her in
> prayer, asking the Lord to bring about complete
> healing and reconciliation.
>
> Signed this _____ day of _____, 20___
>
> _____

If you've already made amends with the family members you've offended, you're not off the hook. *If one of your family members has offended you, it's your move to forgive, even if he or she has not asked for forgiveness.* Forgiveness isn't contingent upon the other person's seeking forgiveness. Rather, we're to have the same attitude as Christ, who cried from the cross: "Father, forgive them; for they do not know what they are doing" (Luke 23:34).

Think back on that time when someone in your family hurt you deeply (your answer on page 82). Have you forgiven that person? Why, or why not?

_____

_____

_____

_____

_____

If you're still nursing that hurt, can you honestly say that you're not in the torturers' prison, emotionally and spiritually? Explain.

_____

_____

_____

_____

_____

Would you like to escape? You can through forgiveness. Will you commit to forgiving that family member who hurt you, regardless of the wound? If so, sign the following contract.

I, _____,
resolve to forgive and no longer hold grudges
against _____
for the offenses described above. I do not expect
_____ to
apologize or otherwise make it up to me, but I will
graciously accept anything that person chooses
to offer. After addressing the problem, I will not
revisit the offenses with others, including the
person who hurt me. I realize that only the grace
of Jesus Christ will heal my wounded spirit and
relieve my resentment. I accept that this may be a
process that takes a long time. Whenever I feel the
need to rehash the wrongs done, I will take them
to the Lord and ask Him to rescue me from the
torturers of unforgiveness and resentment.

Signed this _____ day of _____, 20___

_____

Nothing cuts deeper than hurtful words wielded by those closest to us: our family. Family bruises turn a deeper hue and last longer than any bruises we might receive from an outside bully. And whether we're giving the bruises and cuts or receiving them, the wounds will become infected and fester . . . unless we cover them with the healing balm of forgiveness.

Make no mistake, forgiveness is not given cheaply. And asking for it, particularly from our children, isn't easy. But oh, the treasure it purchases: freedom — freedom for the offender from the fear of vengeance and freedom for the offended from the ever-consuming desire for revenge.

Lesson Ten

Accepting Reproof from Those Who Love Us

Selected Proverbs and Ephesians 6:1–4

THE HEART OF THE MATTER

As we continue to explore biblical parenting, we need to be reminded of the often unmentioned benefits of reproof. No one could deny the benefits of divine reproofs—those corrections from God that we read of in Scripture. God loves those He disciplines (Hebrews 12:5–6); His reproofs give evidence of His love. The same could be said of human reproofs, especially those that come from within our families. How valuable those words of correction from our parents in our growing-up years! And now, how beneficial the loving reproofs between husbands and wives! Unfortunately, those who offer correction often lack understanding and speak without wisdom. Their ill-timed reproofs come out too strong and bring pain rather than benefit. Many of us have the right motives, but we just don't know *how* to reprove one another the way God intended. In this lesson, let's seek to understand the value and process of speaking the truth in love so we might gain—and share, especially with our children—the helpful insight that can remove blind spots and bring about needed change.

DISCOVERING THE WAY

No one desires correction. Correction implies we have been doing something wrong. Further, correction means having our shortcomings scrutinized. It means facing up to what we have done wrong . . . or at least to someone else's idea of what we have done wrong. When correction comes our way, many of us bristle and retreat into a defensive posture. Such experiences remind us that reproof requires care.

As parents, the need to deliver reproof comes upon us regularly. But how do we handle such situations? What does the Bible teach us about the best way to offer correction to our children? Let's start by considering our personal experiences with receiving reproof.

Think about a memorable reproof that you received. Describe the situation.

_____

_____

_____

_____

_____

How was the reproof handled? What did the individual do well? What could have been improved?

_____

_____

_____

_____

_____

Defining the Word *Reproof*

When we reprove, we confront another's attitudes and/or actions that need to be corrected. We refuse to look the other way and ignore the problem just because that person might be under stress or strain.

Reproof assumes that sharing our concerns is good for the people we love and for those whose lives they touch. When done correctly, our reproofs speak the truth in love to the significant people in our lives.

Though many dread reproof, it's not something to anxiously anticipate. Godly reproof avoids caustic criticisms and angry outbursts. Before we reprove someone, we should carefully and prayerfully consider our words. Such an approach dictates that reproof will be a rare occurrence.

Look up the word *reproof* in the dictionary. Write the definition below.

_____

_____

_____

Observing Examples of Reproof in Scripture

Scripture has a great deal to say about reproof. The book of Proverbs speaks to us generally about reproof, while Ephesians speaks specifically to parents and children. Let's survey several verses to get a sense of what the Bible teaches about offering correction to those closest to us.

 Read Proverbs 3:11–12.

The Proverbs teach us that God's love motivates His reproofs (Proverbs 3:11–12). When He corrects us, we know He loves us. He cares enough to give us that moment of pause after we've gone too far. The Proverbs also make it clear that we should accept such reproof. This means that defensiveness in the face of divine reproof is not a proper response. Instead, we should approach God's correction with an attitude of acceptance, even though we all know how difficult that can be.

What direct command does Proverbs 3:11 give?

_____

_____

_____

What reason does Proverbs 3:12 offer for accepting God's correction?

_____

_____

_____

_____

 Read Proverbs 15:5, 10, 31–33.

Proverbs 15 reveals a number of truths about the nature of reproof. The one who regards reproof (or listens to it) will show an abundance of sense (Proverbs 15:5). In other words, when we learn from reproofs, we gain wisdom. Notice too that Proverbs 15:5 contrasts the one who listens to reproof with the one who rejects a father's discipline. Accepting reproof, then, is much like accepting and learning from the discipline handed down by a parent; in both situations, wisdom and good sense result.

Proverbs 15:10 makes clear the tragic consequences that come to those who do not listen to reproof: punishment and early death. Those who cannot accept reproof set themselves on a path toward destruction. Many today have chosen this very path, one on which travelers embrace every possible desire, leaving discipline and correction behind.

In Proverbs 15, not only do we see the positive and negative results of listening to or ignoring reproof, we also see a way to assess the character of others. We can get clearer sense of people based on their responses to reproof. Proverbs 15:31 makes clear that those who listen to reproof end up surrounded by wise people. Wise people flock together. On the other side of the spectrum, ignoring reproof is a result of self-hatred. Those who cast off correction do not have their own best interests in mind.

How would you say Proverbs 15:33 connects to the issue of listening to or ignoring reproof?

_____

_____

_____

_____

We have seen the qualities and results of reproof (or the lack thereof). But what about the process of reproof? *How* should we reprove another? What guidelines can we find in Scripture?

 Read Proverbs 27:6.

Proverbs 27:6 doesn't explicitly mention reproof, but four truths in the verse certainly apply. First, *the one who reproves should be one who loves.* We need to offer correction only to those we know and love — those people we consider good friends or close family, those to whom we are most committed. Because we are involved in the lives of those people, we're in a position to offer meaningful, effective reproof. Rebukes from strangers mean little, but the stinging words of a faithful friend can have a real impact.

Second, *the bruise that's left lingers long after the wounding is over.* We quickly forget strong words from strangers. But when a friend offers reproof, the wound lingers. And that's how it should work — when a friend says something we need to hear, we should remember it. Reproof from a friend brings into our lives a new and lasting truth, but the reproof of a stranger brings only passing discomfort.

Third, *friendship includes the freedom to confront.* Good friends should be able to reprove one another. This goes for family as well. In friendships and family relationships that stretch over the course of many years, correction will certainly be offered at some point, because close connections will eventually reveal previously hidden faults.

Fourth, *words of flattery represent deception, not love.* The "kisses of the enemy" deceive. Many get taken in by flattery, presuming kind words to be signs of real friendship. But when such words don't come with real care and concern, they qualify as mere flattery.

What images does Proverbs 25:11–12 use to illustrate well-spoken words?

Focus on 25:12. How do you think a reproof is like an earring or an ornament?

As friends and close family members, we ought to correct one another, but before we follow the impulse to reprove, we would do well to observe three guidelines: *reprove in private, never in public; reprove with words designed to correct, never to condemn;* and *reprove at the right time.*

Read Ephesians 6:1–4.

In Ephesians 6, the apostle Paul offered valuable instruction for the parent-child relationship, instruction that we can apply to the topic of reproof. Paul taught that children have two responsibilities: "obey your parents" and "honor your father and mother" (Ephesians 6:1–2). Paul's reasoning for these commands is simple: obedience to parents is the right thing to do, and honoring parents leads to life going well. When children relate to their parents in these ways, parental reproof will have a positive, growth-inducing impact on their lives.

This passage also lays out a responsibility for parents—fathers in particular. Fathers should not provoke their children to anger (6:4). Anger in children does not produce the desired effect. The listening ears of children vanish amidst their anger and frustration. Therefore, fathers need to take care to restrain their personal anger as they bring up their children in the discipline of the Lord. In other words, parents' reproofs should encourage their children to act in accordance with what God wants—to respond correctly in order to please Him, not simply to avoid parental anger. We want our children to do the right thing because they love the ways of the Lord, not because they are trying to abate our anger.

Ephesians 6:2–3 is a quotation from Exodus 20:12, among the Ten Commandments. What do these verses say the result will be for those who honor their fathers and mothers?

_____

_____

_____

_____

Why do you think honoring one's father and mother leads to a long life?

_____

_____

_____

_____

_____

Using Wisdom When We Reprove Others

When we reprove, we need to apply wisdom to the situation. We must stop to _think and pray before saying anything._ Such pause will help ensure that the words we speak are accurate and given in a properly redemptive spirit. Also, we need to remember that _there's no need to share the reproof with anyone else._ Telling others about a reproof offered privately shows disrespect to the reproved, not to mention how playing the gossip impugns our own character. Finally, _as changes occur, affirm, affirm, affirm._ When we offer correction to our children, the change may not come right away. But when it does, we as parents must be ready to affirm and encourage our children in their pursuit of better living.

 STARTING YOUR JOURNEY
What benefits does giving reproof offer? First, _those receiving reproof will know how much you love them._ If the reproofs you offer your friends, children, and other family members are truly given with of a heart of concern, the people who receive them will understand the care behind them. Second, _your reproof will cause the person's respect for you to increase._ Not only will your care be unmistakable, but the one receiving reproof will hold you in higher regard.

Have you ever offered reproof to a friend or a child? How did it go?

_____

_____

_____

_____

Having studied the Scripture passages in this lesson, do you think your reproof could have gone better? How?

_____

_____

_____

_____

Is there anyone you need to reprove now? If so, write down some ideas about how to approach the situation.

_____

_____

_____

_____

Offering correction to a child—and doing it well—has to be one of the toughest tasks for any parent. However, Scripture makes it clear that reproof is an essential element of the parent-child relationship and, for that matter, of any close relationship. We must reprove, and we must be reproved. Scripture also makes it clear that reproof must be offered carefully and thoughtfully. We can easily be consumed by anger, frustration, or exasperation. Effective reproof, however, is free of all these things. Therefore, we must be steady and intentional in our approach to correction. We must meditate on Scripture. We must prayerfully consider our words. Only then will we find success in correcting our children and putting them back on the path of discipline in the Lord.

Lesson Eleven

Suggestions for Parenting Grown-Up Kids

Ephesians 4:25–32

 THE HEART OF THE MATTER

Living harmoniously as a family is an ongoing, intentional journey. The beginning of that journey is marked by great anticipation and genuine excitement. A bride and groom have high hopes and great dreams as they start out life together. However, as in all journeys, unexpected challenges pop up, including the arrival of children, which requires the couple to cultivate valuable parenting skills—without a handbook! At each age, from preschool through elementary school, each child requires his or her parents to make adjustments along the way to keep the relationships harmonious. Just about the time parents get their arms around all of that, the teenage years arrive! This stretching and complicated time calls for even more adjustments and a greater willingness to change if the parents hope to sustain harmony in the home. Then, after all that adapting, a brand new set of challenges arrives—the children reach adulthood, with minds of their own. Can there still be mutual respect and meaningful relationships in the family? Can harmony continue between parents and their grown-up kids? Absolutely! The question is, *How?*

 DISCOVERING THE WAY

Most books on parenting make little to no mention of parenting adult children. What unique challenges come with being the parent of adult children? What opportunities do parents of adult children have? At the very least, making it through the childhoods and adolescences of our children has bestowed on us the humility that comes through experience. We once thought we had it all figured out, but decades of parenting have taught us that we still have so much to learn. Such humility can be extremely valuable as we seek to relate to our adult children.

How would you characterize your relationship with your adult children?

_____

_____

_____

_____

_____

Describe your relationship with your parents as you moved into adulthood. What challenges cropped up? What joys appeared?

_____

_____

_____

_____

_____

Relational Essentials That Must Never Change

For every family, there exists a baseline of how things are supposed to function. These relational essentials do not change, but too often, they pass under a family's radar. Bringing these essentials to the surface at the outset of this lesson will help provide some boundaries for interacting with adult children.

First of all, *no challenge in any family is impossible.* Some families face what seem like unbearable trials. In these moments, we sense the walls closing in, cutting off any route of escape. Whether the challenge involves poor health, unbecoming behavior, or one of any number of other difficulties, we can easily feel boxed in. However, we know from Scripture that nothing is impossible with God (Luke 1:37). He can deal with even the darkest of circumstances—a truth we know from His work throughout history, as recorded in Scripture.

Read Exodus 14:5–14. Describe the situation the Israelites were in.

_____

_____

_____

_____

How did the people respond to their circumstances?

_____

_____

_____

_____

How did God (through Moses) respond to the people?

_____

_____

_____

_____

Without God's intervention, what do you think would have happened to the Israelites?

_____

_____

_____

_____

Second, *no child of any age is in authority.* Just because children grow into adults does not mean they take on authority over their parents. No. Adult children must still respect and honor their parents as parents. This requires forgiving past wrongs and persevering through current disagreements. Parents always retain their position of honor and respect, even as children grow up and make life decisions for themselves.

Third, *no person in the family is independent of other family members.* We can compare our families to bodies, with living parts joined together to form a whole. Each part has particular needs of its own, but all the parts only thrive when they work together to ensure the body's general needs are met. Likewise, family members are all interrelated. The actions of one impact all the others. Family members, even adult children, therefore, should not see themselves as isolated figures whose actions don't impact their parents and siblings. No one is truly independent.

Fourth, *no reaction to any issue should be handled in the flesh.* In other words, don't be reactionary. When we respond impulsively, we open the door to acting in ways contrary to the Lord's desires for us. With quick, in-the-moment reactions, we often jump to conclusions and make dogmatic statements based on faulty conclusions. This only fosters problems and creates landmines in our relationships with our children. Rather, we need to step back, consider what the Lord would have us do, and respond appropriately.

Read Galatians 5:13–24. With what did Paul contrast living according to the flesh?

_____

_____

What specific activities did Paul associate with living according to the flesh?

_____

_____

_____

_____

Which item on the list do you think would be most tempting for average parents to indulge as they deal with their children? Explain your answer.

_____

_____

_____

_____

Biblical Principles That Should Always Be Followed

While the Bible doesn't say much that explicitly relates to grown children, it does teach us a great deal about our relationships with other people, and we can apply those truths to our relationships with our adult children. As we examine a passage from Paul's epistle to the Ephesians, we will uncover six, two-word principles that we should incorporate into our interactions with our adult children.

Read Ephesians 4:25–32.

Number one: *speak truth.* Grown-up children deserve to hear the truth from their parents. Paul's exhortation to Christians involves laying aside falsehood. Parents of small children don't need to lie, but they do often need to keep back certain information. And rightly so. Small children are not always ready to hear every dark detail. However, as our children grow older, they can handle more and, therefore, we tell them more. And when they reach adulthood? Choose an appropriate time and tell it straight. This applies to issues related to family history, reproofs our adult children need to hear, and a host of other circumstances. Whatever the case, our children deserve the truth.

Number two: *be passionate.* Or to say it another way, don't be passive. Homes are filled with passive parents, people who yawn through their kids' growing-up years and then wonder why their kids turned out the way they did. Ephesians 4:26 commands us to "be angry"—not in a way that gives the devil an opportunity to tempt our family members but in a way that accords with righteousness. Our children need to see that we care about things! They need to know that certain issues get our blood boiling and create opportunities for us to point each other in the right direction—not out of uncontrollable rage but out of our straightforward rejection of and hatred for that which is evil in this world. At times, our anger will be directed outward beyond our homes. At other times, we will find the evil in our families (which includes ourselves). Our honesty about and passionate response to evil will instruct our adult children as they continually refine their approach to the world and to their own families.

Read Judges 2:20–22. Describe God's demeanor in this passage.

_____

_____

_____

_____

What reason did God offer to explain His anger?

_____

_____

_____

_____

What was the ultimate purpose behind God's anger?

_____

_____

_____

_____

How do you think God's anger in this passage can be instructive for a parent of grown children?

_____

_____

_____

_____

Number three: *stop stealing*. How can we apply Paul's warning about stealing to our relationships with our adult children (Ephesians 4:28)? We can stop stealing their freedom to make decisions on their own. We steal freedom from our children when we meddle in their affairs, don't allow them to be adults, and prevent them from making their own way in the world. When we involve ourselves too heavily in the decision-making of our children, we stunt their growth. Even as adults, our children still have growing to do. We need to let them live their lives so that they can mature into the people God made them to be.

Number four: *stop yelling*. Any time a parent feels the need to yell at an adult child, that parent has lost control. Paul exhorted believers to make sure not to let any unwholesome word proceed from our mouths (Ephesians 4:29). Yelling counts as unwholesome talk. When we yell, threaten, curse, or use sarcasm, we fail to communicate effectively with our children. And we can rest assured that they will not hear what we are trying to communicate.

Number five: *give grace*. Children make mistakes when they're young. They continue to make mistakes when they grow into adults. Mistakes are a regular part of life, and so we should not be surprised when our children make them. Paul encouraged God's people to speak words of edification that will give grace to those who hear (4:29). When we speak to our grown children, especially in the aftermath of their errors, we need to speak words that communicate grace by building up and encouraging our children.

What did Paul prohibit in Ephesians 4:29?

_____

_____

_____

_____

What did Paul contrast with unwholesome words in that same verse?

_____

_____

_____

_____

What unwholesome words do you think are especially tempting for a parent of grown children to use?

_____

_____

_____

_____

Number six: *be kind.* Everyone yearns for kindness. We thrive on it. It sustains us through difficult times. Kindness requires us to be willing to forgive our children when they fall short in our relationships with them. Kindness also requires us as parents to receive our children's forgiveness when we fall short ourselves.

 DIGGING DEEPER
Forging a Life of Forgiveness
We do well to praise God and to celebrate Christ's free offer of grace in salvation. However, at times, our minds become so focused on that initial event that we end up forgetting about the long, hard road of living the Christian life. Ephesians 4:31–32 offers Christians significant insight into how to live in the body of Christ. If we focus only on the beginning of our lives in Christ, we might think being a Christian isn't all that difficult. However, Paul reminded us how difficult it can be.

As Christians, we have been called to forgive one another. The need for forgiveness implies that some wrong has been committed or pain has been caused. When we allow hurt to dictate our actions, we become separated from our fellow believers and lost in the bitterness and malice of unforgiveness. Being a vital part of Christ's body, then, requires a life committed to forgiveness. This is not a onetime act or something we can check off a list. Forgiveness must be a regular part of our lives if we expect to make a lasting impact for Christ.

STARTING YOUR JOURNEY
How can parents of adult children use the list we've created from Ephesians 4? First, *memorize it*. When we commit things to memory, we greatly increase our chances of actually using them in our daily lives.

Second, *share it with someone else*. Talk about this list with others. Not only will it give other parents more exposure to things they should be doing, but it will further solidify the list in our own minds.

Finally, *enjoy the benefits*. When we treat our children in the godly fashion outlined in Ephesians 4, we can better enjoy the time we spend with them. And as they mature, we'll find that they want to spend time with us too.

How are you doing with the list of six, two-word principles outlined in Ephesians? Which of the six do you most often practice in your relationships with your children?

_____

_____

_____

_____

Which of the six do you practice the least often in your relationships with your children?

_____

_____

_____

_____

Take a few minutes right now to pray for your relationships with your children. Write a summary of that prayer on the lines below.

_____

_____

_____

_____

Parents want to have good relationships with their kids. That desire strengthens as our children move from childhood to adulthood. As you ponder the relationships you have with your children, remember to focus on that list of six from Ephesians 4: speak truth, be passionate, stop stealing, stop yelling, give grace, and be kind. Each time you speak with or visit your adult children, make these things a reality in your relationships with them. The presence of good things like these softens hearts—both yours and theirs—and makes the way for meaningful relationships easier than ever.

Lesson Twelve

What to Do When You've Blown It
Isaiah 58:6–12; Joel 2:23–26

THE HEART OF THE MATTER
We've come to the end of our study of biblical parenting. It's been a journey of discovery! We've probed Scripture from start to finish to find out what God thinks about this all-important subject. We've learned skills to enhance the vital relationships within our homes and families. We've covered a broad spectrum—from embryos in their mothers' wombs to grown, adult kids. And we have relied on God's Word to guide our thinking. While we're grateful for biblical instruction, there are times it can be very disquieting, especially when we realize how we have failed to do things God's way. Too often, we end up saying, "If only I had known *then* what I know *now*." How deep the feelings of regret and anxiety in the hearts of parents who "blew it"! Since there's no way to go back and relive our lives, we need to focus on the best way to respond to these painful memories. Otherwise, we will live under clouds of blame and shame and be paralyzed by fear.

DISCOVERING THE WAY
The guilt of a parent who has made mistakes can linger for years on end. Moms and dads struggling with guilt often feel stuck in a downward spiral with little sense of how to break free. Long-lasting shame creates decay in us, and as parents, that decay spreads into our relationships with our children. How can we overcome such guilt? Is there even any hope of overcoming it?

List a few mistakes you have made in parenting your children.

_____

_____

_____

_____

_____

_____

How have those mistakes impacted you since you made them?

_____

_____

_____

_____

_____

_____

Painful Realities of Being Human

Reality makes clear that certain qualities and experiences are common to all of us. Parents need to recognize especially three painful realities that can help address feelings of undue guilt and shame.

First, *we are all imperfect—including our kids*. The apostle Paul made this point abundantly clear when he declared that we have all sinned (Romans 3:23). We know this truth from Scripture, but we know it from experience as well. People don't walk around believing that they have lived perfect lives. However, we forget this reality about ourselves and others—including our children. And when we forget, we end up burdened by undue guilt and shame.

Everyone feels guilt over sinful deeds. But repentance and God's forgiveness cover that guilt. Many parents struggle with excessive guilt, either because they've not repented before God or because they have forgotten His forgiveness.

Second, *we cannot change the past.* What has already happened is set in stone. It will not change. And yet, so many of us desire to go back in time—at least in our minds. Retracing the same mistakes over and over and trying to make them less than they were is only a waste of time. We must press on beyond our failures, mistakes, and sins, embracing reality for what it is while trying to mature ourselves and improve our relationships as they are now.

Third, *we are personally responsible for our own wrongs.* We all face the temptation to minimize our faults or push the blame on someone else. This tendency comes naturally, and extends back to our ancestors in the garden of Eden (Genesis 3:11–12). As parents, we have to recognize our own responsibility in the raising of our kids. It is easy to blame them, their schools, the church, or society in general. But, while all of those influences have an impact on how our kids turn out, we must not avoid a clear-eyed look in the mirror. We must be honest about what we as parents have done—both good and bad—in the raising of our kids.

Read Jeremiah 29:11–13. What message did God give Israel?

How can this message of hope speak to the plight of parents struggling with guilt about choices they have made in bringing up their children?

_____

_____

_____

_____

While we all must recognize our frailties, the unchanging nature of the past, and our responsibility for what we have done, we should not be a people without hope. As believers in the true God, we know that He has a future planned for us despite our past failures. The same was true for God's people in the Old Testament era.

 Read Joel 2:23–26.

In the Old Testament, Joel prophesied the coming of a mighty army that will overrun the Promised Land, an army of judgment upon the disobedient people of God (Joel 2:1–11). However, in the midst of this prophecy of judgment, God also spoke hope through His prophet. He called the people to repentance (2:12), exhorting them not to be afraid (2:21). Though suffering would come for this people, God wanted them to remember that there will be a good future for them as well. With that hope in mind, God called the people to rejoice (2:23). Though a trial stood before them, God wanted the people focused on their ultimate future.

Fear, especially fear spurred by guilt over past actions, can paralyze parents. Fear freezes even the most active of people. As a people of hope, believers have no business living in fear. Sure, we all struggle with it at times. But we must always strive to overcome it, to live as people of hope in a world pushing us to fear.

What is the ultimate promise that God offered in Joel 2:26?

_____

_____

_____

_____

How might that promise inspire parents struggling with guilt over their past actions?

_____

_____

_____

_____

Moving from Guilt and Shame to Recovery and Renewal

How do the parents among God's people move from guilt and shame to recovery and renewal? We can answer this question both negatively and positively. First, let's look at two negatives.

It won't help to misunderstand biblical instruction. We need to be astute students of God's Word, with a clear understanding of who He expects us to be. Parents have a responsibility to teach their children the ways of God. The Lord made clear through His apostle what it looks like to bear the fruit of the Spirit; therefore, parents are responsible for making sure their children understand what it means to love, to be joyful, to be peaceful, and so on (Galatians 5:22–23).

However, if we misunderstand God's Word, we will misapply biblical instruction and lead our children astray. If we teach our kids that Christianity is all about rule-following and the harsh judgment of others, we'll leave them with a misunderstanding of the faith—one that lacks grace and humility. As parents, then, we need to make every effort to understand God's Word so that we can lead our children well.

It won't help to ignore common sense. With so many activities and concerns pulling at our attention, many parents seem to have forgotten plain old common sense, leaving them baffled when their kids go off the rails. Parents do a thankless job that sometimes requires some hard common sense tasks, including strong talk, reproof, honest confrontation, standing ground, and setting boundaries. None of this work is easy, but it is essential, for when we ignore the common sense tasks, we expose our children to lives of increasingly alluring temptations.

 Read Isaiah 58:6–12.

Now, let's look at the other side of the ledger, where we find five positive tasks to help us move from guilt and shame to recovery and renewal. First, *humble yourself* (Isaiah 58:7–8). Pride plays a vital role in nearly all sin. In our homes, pride keeps us silent. Pride keeps us from going and making things right. Pride leaves us with fragmented families. However, humility leaves us with nothing to prove and nothing to lose. When we approach our family members in a spirit of humility, we show them that our goal is to be one with them, rather than to prove ourselves right.

What examples of humble behavior does Isaiah 58:7 offer?

_____

_____

_____

_____

What is the result of humble behavior, according to Isaiah 58:8?

_____

_____

_____

_____

Second, *recovery and renewal will come when we pray* (Isaiah 58:9). We need to pray more than just, "God help me!" Our children deserve for us to go before the Father and offer real prayers, ones that bring them before Him and seek out His wisdom and direction for dealing with past mistakes and present pain and guilt within our families.

Third, *stop all blaming.* Isaiah 58:9 includes the phrase "remove the yoke." The idea behind it? Stop with all the finger-pointing! We need to look carefully at our own problems and recognize that most often they are not the results of others' actions but the results of our own sin. If we will refuse to walk around our homes blaming everyone else, we will remove a heavy yoke from those closest to us. We will allow them to live in a freeing space, where recovery and renewal can occur.

Fourth, *make yourself available and vulnerable* (58:10–11). Our children need us, and they need to know we are there for them. When we make ourselves available, we give them the precious gift of ourselves. Though we are flawed and broken, there will never be anyone in a child's life with as much potential to make a meaningful impact as an available and vulnerable parent. Such a reality could make all the difference for a child.

What actions does God require of His people, according to Isaiah 58:10?

_____

_____

_____

_____

What does the passage say will result from taking those actions?

_____

_____

_____

_____

How do you think a parent's availability and vulnerability shine like a light that casts away gloom from a family?

_____

_____

_____

_____

Finally, *trust God to bring healing and change* (Isaiah 58:12). This passage in Isaiah speaks of rebuilt ancient ruins—a wonderful image to apply to a family that has been broken by its members' sins against one another. God loves healing. He loves redeeming broken vessels and putting them back together again. We see this truth throughout Scripture, and we see it all around us. Therefore, we have every reason to trust in His faithfulness.

Some of the barriers to recovery and renewal within our families have been there a long time. Following the five positive tasks outlined above likely won't break down all the barriers at once. However, these actions, practiced over and over, will strengthen the bonds of any family, making the way for true healing.

STARTING YOUR JOURNEY

We must recognize that change is a process. Moving from guilt and shame toward recovery and renewal is no exception. It takes time. As we seek to make positive changes in the relationships we have with our children, we need to keep in mind the following three tips.

Number one: *don't hide anything.* We need to be straight with our children, especially when we have failed them. We cannot hide our behavior behind some kind of "parental privilege." Our children need us to be open about our failures so they have the opportunity to grapple with reality and grow.

Number two: *don't hurry the process.* We might think otherwise, but we don't need closure right away. Pushing for an immediate end to any negative situation shows our children that the exchange we're having with them is more about us than them. We need to give them the space to deal with the bad news and forgive us from the fullness of their hearts, whenever they decide to do that.

Number three: *don't hold on to the past.* Don't bring up the issue again. We have a habit of treading back over the same mistakes, time and again. Rather than being helpful, this is merely a way for us to wallow in our own guilt. Once we speak our minds and offer our apologies, we need to leave that issue in the past where it belongs.

Consider the parenting mistakes you previously listed. Have you engaged your children about these issues? If so, were you completely honest?

_____

_____

_____

_____

Did your children immediately forgive you, or has it been a process of healing that has taken time? What positive results have you seen because of your confession?

_____

_____

_____

_____

_____

Has it been a struggle for you to avoid bringing up these issues again? If so, when do they seem to come up? Why do you think that is?

_____

_____

_____

_____

_____

_____

If you have made a mistake with your children and have not yet addressed the issue with them, give some thought and prayer to apologizing and putting the issue behind you. Summarize your prayer on the lines below.

_____

_____

_____

_____

Everyone makes mistakes. When we look at the nature of relationships in our fallen world, we see that we *are* going to hurt others. It's inevitable. And often, the people we hurt the most are those closest to us. But when we look at the nature of God, we see that He restores what has been broken. He makes all things new. God loves to do that. We, too, should love to restore as He does. And who better to work with on renewal than our own children, those special people God placed in our hands to love, guide, instruct, and cherish for the rest of our days? May we all find strength and renewal as we continue to commit ourselves to His Word and seek to be the biblical parents He intends us to be.

How to Begin a Relationship with God

We have in God the perfect Father. As parents ourselves, we can appreciate the deep, unrelenting love that He has for His children. We can identify with the joy He experiences when His children live in harmony with their design. And we can empathize with His sorrow when His children choose rebellion over intimacy with Him.

No relationship means as much as our bond with God the Father. Our interactions with other people—including our children—can never be completely whole unless this primary relationship is right. But because of sin, for each of us, that relationship begins broken. The good news is, restoration is possible—God has made a way. The Bible marks the path with four essential truths. Let's look at each marker in detail.

Our Spiritual Condition: Totally Depraved

The first truth is rather personal. One look in the mirror of Scripture, and our human condition becomes painfully clear:

> "There is none righteous, not even one;
> There is none who understands,
> There is none who seeks for God;
> All have turned aside, together they have become
>   useless;
> There is none who does good,
> There is not even one." (Romans 3:10–12)

We are all sinners through and through—totally depraved. Now, that doesn't mean we've committed every atrocity known to human-kind. We're not as *bad* as we can be, just as *bad off* as we can be. Sin colors all our thoughts, motives, words, and actions.

If you've been around a while, you likely already believe it. Look around. Everything around us bears the smudge marks of our sinful nature. Despite our best efforts to create a perfect world, crime statistics continue to soar, divorce rates keep climbing, and families keep crumbling.

Something has gone terribly wrong in our society and in ourselves—something deadly. Contrary to how the world would repackage it, "me-first" living doesn't equal rugged individuality and freedom; it equals death. As Paul said in his letter to the Romans, "The wages of sin is death" (Romans 6:23)—our spiritual and physical death that comes from God's righteous judgment of our sin, along with all of the emotional and practical effects of this separation that we experience on a daily basis. This brings us to the second marker: God's character.

God's Character: Infinitely Holy

How can God judge us for a sinful state we were born into? Our total depravity is only half the answer. The other half is God's infinite holiness.

The fact that we know things are not as they should be points us to a standard of goodness beyond ourselves. Our sense of injustice in life on this side of eternity implies a perfect standard of justice beyond our reality. That standard and source is God Himself. And God's standard of holiness contrasts starkly with our sinful condition.

Scripture says that "God is Light, and in Him there is no darkness at all" (1 John 1:5). God is absolutely holy—which creates a problem for us. If He is so pure, how can we who are so impure relate to Him?

Perhaps we could try being better people, try to tilt the balance in favor of our good deeds, or seek out methods for self-improvement. Throughout history, people have attempted to live up to God's standard by keeping the Ten Commandments or living by their own code of ethics. Unfortunately, no one can come close to satisfying the demands of God's law. Romans 3:20 says, "By the works of the Law no flesh will be justified in His sight; for through the Law comes the knowledge of sin."

Our Need: A Substitute

So here we are, sinners by nature and sinners by choice, trying to pull ourselves up by our own bootstraps to attain a relationship with our holy Creator. But every time we try, we fall flat on our faces. We can't live a good enough life to make up for our sin, because God's standard isn't "good enough" — it's *perfection*. And we can't make amends for the offense our sin has created without dying for it.

Who can get us out of this mess?

If someone could live perfectly, honoring God's law, and would bear sin's death penalty for us — in our place — then we would be saved from our predicament. But is there such a person? Thankfully, yes!

Meet your substitute — *Jesus Christ*. He is the One who took death's place for you!

> [God] made [Jesus Christ] who knew no sin to be sin on our behalf, so that we might become the righteousness of God in Him. (2 Corinthians 5:21)

God's Provision: A Savior

God rescued us by sending His Son, Jesus, to die on the cross for our sins (1 John 4:9–10). Jesus was fully human and fully divine (John 1:1, 18), a truth that ensures His understanding of our weaknesses, His power to forgive, and His ability to bridge the gap between God and us (Romans 5:6–11). In short, we are "justified as a gift by His grace through the redemption which is in Christ Jesus" (Romans 3:24). Two words in this verse bear further explanation: *justified* and *redemption*.

Justification is God's act of mercy, in which He declares righteous the believing sinners while we are still in our sinning state. Justification doesn't mean that God *makes* us righteous, so that we never sin again, rather that He *declares* us righteous—much like a judge pardons a guilty criminal. Because Jesus took our sin upon Himself and suffered our judgment on the cross, God forgives our debt and proclaims us PARDONED.

Redemption is Christ's act of paying the complete price to release us from sin's bondage. God sent His Son to bear His wrath for all of our sins—past, present, and future (Romans 3:24–26; 2 Corinthians 5:21). In humble obedience, Christ willingly endured the shame of the cross for our sake (Mark 10:45; Romans 5:6–8; Philippians 2:8). Christ's death satisfied God's righteous demands. He no longer holds our sins against us, because His own Son paid the penalty for them. We are freed from the slave market of sin, never to be enslaved again!

Placing Your Faith in Christ

These four truths describe how God has provided a way to Himself through Jesus Christ. Because the price has been paid in full by God, we must respond to His free gift of eternal life in total faith and confidence in Him to save us. We must step forward into the relationship with God that He has prepared for us—not by doing good works or by being a good person, but by coming to Him just as we are and accepting His justification and redemption by faith.

> For by grace you have been saved through faith;
> and that not of yourselves, it is the gift of God;
> not as a result of works, so that no one may boast.
> (Ephesians 2:8–9)

We accept God's gift of salvation simply by placing our faith in Christ alone for the forgiveness of our sins. Would you like to enter a relationship with your Creator by trusting in Christ as your Savior? If so, here's a simple prayer you can use to express your faith:

Dear God,

I know that my sin has put a barrier between You and me.
Thank You for sending Your Son, Jesus, to die in my place.
I trust in Jesus alone to forgive my sins, and I accept His
gift of eternal life. I ask Jesus to be my personal Savior and
the Lord of my life. Thank You. In Jesus's name, amen.

If you've prayed this prayer or one like it and you wish to find out more about knowing God and His plan for you in the Bible, contact us at Insight for Living Ministries. Our contact information is on the following pages.

We Are Here for You

If you desire to find out more about knowing God and His plan for you in the Bible, contact us. Insight for Living Ministries provides staff pastors who are available for free written correspondence or phone consultation. These seminary-trained and seasoned counselors have years of experience and are well-qualified guides for your spiritual journey.

Please feel welcome to contact your regional office by using the information below:

United States
Insight for Living
Biblical Counseling Department
Post Office Box 269000
Plano, Texas 75026-9000
USA
972-473-5097 (Monday through Friday,
8:00 a.m.–5:00 p.m. central time)
www.insight.org/contactapastor

Canada
Insight for Living Canada
Biblical Counseling Department
PO Box 8 Stn A
Abbotsford BC   V2T 6Z4
CANADA
1-800-663-7639
info@insightforliving.ca

Australia, New Zealand, and South Pacific
Insight for Living Australia
Pastoral Care
Post Office Box 443
Boronia, VIC 3155
AUSTRALIA
1300 467 444

United Kingdom and Europe
Insight for Living United Kingdom
Pastoral Care
PO Box 553
Dorking
RH4 9EU
UNITED KINGDOM
0800 787 9364
+44 (0)1306 640156
pastoralcare@insightforliving.org.uk

Endnotes

Unless otherwise noted below, all material in this Bible Companion is adapted from the *Biblical Parenting* sermon series by Charles R. Swindoll and was supplemented by the Creative Ministries Department of Insight for Living.

Lesson One

1. Francis Brown, S. R. Driver, and Charles A. Briggs, *The Brown-Driver-Briggs Hebrew and English Lexicon* (Peabody, Mass.: Hendrickson, 2006), 335.

Lesson Six

1. Fyodor Dostoevsky, "The Latest Literary Controversies," in *Dostoevsky's Occasional Writings*, trans. David Magarshack (Evanston, Ill: Northwestern University Press, 1997), 214.

Lesson Eight

1. Albert Camus, *The Rebel: An Essay on Man in Revolt*, trans. Anthony Bower (New York: Vintage Books, 1956), 13.

2. John White, *Parents in Pain: A Book of Comfort and Counsel* (Downers Grove, Ill.: InterVarsity, 1979), 201.

3. C. S. Lewis, *The Problem of Pain*, in *The Complete C. S. Lewis Signature Classics* (San Francisco: HarperSanFrancisco, 2002), 407.

Lesson Nine

1. Texas Bix Bender, *Don't Squat with Yer Spurs On! A Cowboy's Guide to Life* (Layton, Utah: Gibbs Smith, 1992), 13.

2. Os Guinness, *Unspeakable: Facing Up to Evil in an Age of Genocide and Terror* (San Francisco: HarperSanFrancisco, 2005), 178.

3. *Merriam-Webster's Collegiate Dictionary*, 11th ed. (Springfield, Mass.: Merriam-Webster, 2007), "forgive."

4. See Frederick William Danker, ed., *A Greek-English Lexicon of the New Testament and Other Early Christian Literature*, 3d rev. ed. (Chicago: University of Chicago Press, 2000), 168.

Resources for Probing Further

Whether we are just getting started or have been parents for decades, we all need help parenting God's way. Hopefully, your time spent in the *Biblical Parenting Bible Companion* has given you the truths you need to parent well. As you continue on, you may want to further your study of the subject, and there are many excellent resources to help you do just that. Of course, we cannot always endorse everything a writer or ministry says, so we encourage you to approach these and all other non-biblical resources with wisdom and discernment.

Boggs, Tamara. *And Then God Gave Us Kids: How God Uses Our Kids to Help Us Grow*. Grand Rapids: Kregel, 2003.

Dobson, James. *The New Dare to Discipline*. Wheaton, Ill.: Tyndale House, 1996.

Insight for Living. *You and Your Daughter: A LifeMaps Book*. Plano, Tex.: IFL Publishing House, 2007.

Swindoll, Charles R. *Parenting: From Surviving to Thriving*. Nashville: W Publishing, 2006.

Swindoll, Charles R. *Parenting: From Surviving to Thriving Workbook*. Nashville: W Publishing, 2006.

Swindoll, Charles R. *The Strong Family*. Grand Rapids: Zondervan, 1991.

Swindoll, Charles R. *When God's Gift Comes Specially Wrapped*. Plano, Tex.: IFL Publishing House, 2007.

Tripp, Tedd. *Shepherding Your Child's Heart*. Wapwallopen, Pa.: Shepherd Press, 1995.